Mary
Wyllie

HUNT BADGES

NEWRY
HARRIERS

ROYAL ROCK
BEAGLES

BELVOIR
FOXHOUNDS

DUKE OF
BUCCLEUGH'S

NEW FOREST
BUCKHOUNDS

DUNSTON
HARRIERS

BICESTER AND W...
HILL FOXHOU...

Acknowledgements

The publishers gratefully acknowledge the generous co-operation of many horse societies, organisations and hunts.

Photographs were kindly supplied by:—

    Monty
    Reed Photography
    Sport and General
    Radio Times Hulton Picture Library
    Mirrorpic

Made and printed in Great Britain by Clarke & Sherwell Ltd., Kingsthorpe, Northampton, and London. This book may only be exported for sale in the following territories by the appointed sole agents: AUSTRALIA—Ponsford, Newman & Benson, Ltd. NEW ZEALAND—Whitcombe & Tombs, Ltd. AFRICA—Purnell & Sons (S.A.) (Pty) Ltd.

The Dumpy Pocket Book of
RIDING AND SHOW JUMPING

by

CAPTAIN G. H. S. WEBBER

Secretary General of The British Show Jumping Association

and

C. P. STRATTON

Assistant Secretary General of The British Show Jumping Association

Assistant Editor: Patricia A. King

SAMPSON LOW · LONDON

© 1961

Sampson Low, Marston & Co. Ltd.

CONTENTS

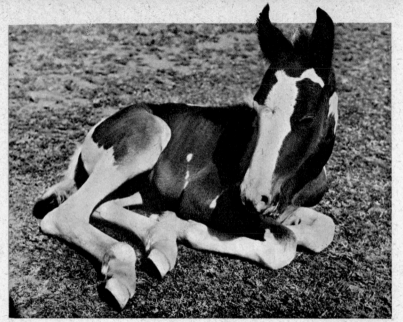

In the beginning . . .

CHAPTER ONE

The Evolution of the Horse

The horse has become so much a part of man's life that often when people try to imagine how the horse appeared in the past they conjure up a picture of a proud charger clad in chain mail, and being used in battles both as a form of transport and also for jousting in towns and villages.

However, all this occurred when the horse had developed considerably, and its appearance then was very much as it is today. In order to trace the original ancestor we have to go back many millions of years and then we find a four-toed creature known as a *Hyracotherium*, which was about the size of a hare. This animal gradually developed and became known as the *Mesohippus*. After several million years this developed into the *Merrychippus* and finally to the *Pliohippus*, which was about the size of a Shetland Pony. Then from this was developed the *Equus*, an animal which walked on one toe only, as indeed the horse today still does. Direct descendants of these early horses may still be found in Mongolia today.

Prehistoric man hunted the horse for his flesh in the same way that man now hunts deer. In some countries, particularly France and Belgium, there is still a considerable demand for horse flesh for human consumption.

The first records showing that man was interested in the horse were in paintings discovered on the walls of caves in Spain and in the Sahara, these paintings showed the wild horses which wandered all over the European and Asian plains.

The horse, a very swift animal, was not imprisoned and domesticated, until many years after such animals as the dog, the ox and the ass.

The first known reference to man riding a horse is made in the Second Book of Kings, when *Rabshakeh* said to *Hezekiah*, the King of Judah, "I will deliver thee two thousand horses if thou be able on thy part to set riders upon them."

As early as the ninth century B.C.

A palaeolithic cave painting showing a deer superimposed on what appears to be a horse.

The Godolphin Arabian.

horses were used for pulling chariots both in war and for sport. Chariot racing was a popular sport and a regular feature of the Greek and Roman Games. This was the fore-runner of the trotting races which are held throughout the world today. Oliver Cromwell, who was not only a great politician, but also a great General, first perceived the idea of using cavalry in war, and this is the picture that is generally thought of today.

For man was quite content to use the horse as a beast of burden, and did not consider for many years improvements which could be made in the breeding of the animal. In fact it was William the Conqueror who imported a number of

The Darley Arabian.

The Byerley Turk.

horses from Spain and said that they were far too noble to be used for pulling ploughs and suchlike work, and he ordered that this work should be done by oxen.

The foundations for the English thoroughbred that we know today, were laid in the eighteenth century with the importation of three famous stallions, the Darley Arabian, the Byerley Turk and the Godolphin Arabian or Barb.

11

The horse has always been the constant companion of man whether it be in peace or in war. He has carried him on pilgrimages, he has carried him on hunting expeditions, he has been used as a method of transport, both being ridden and pulling coaches and waggons, and in the present day he plays a major part in the world of sport.

Probably the finest tribute which has been written to the horse, are the words written by Ronald Duncan, and which are read at the closing ceremony of the Horse of the Year Show each year.

"Where in this wide world can man find nobility without pride, friendship without envy or beauty without vanity? Here, where grace is laced with muscle, and strength by gentleness confined.

He serves without servility; he has fought without enmity. There is nothing so powerful, nothing less violent, there is nothing so quick, nothing more patient.

England's past has been borne on his back. All our history is his industry; we are his heirs, he our inheritance."

CHAPTER TWO

Types of Horses and Ponies

Heavy or Working Horses. There are four recognised breeds of Heavy Horses: Clydesdale, Percheron, Shire and Suffolk Punch.

CLYDESDALES first bred in Scotland, probably by cross breeding with English and Flemish heavy horses. Speed and length of stride, bone structure and general hardiness make them excellent for agricultural purposes. They stand at 16 to 16.2 hands and are generally bay or dark brown though other colours are not uncommon. A white blaze, star, or stripe is usually present on the face and the legs are often completely or partially white as well. The Breed Society is the *Clydesdale Society, 19 Hillington Gardens, Glasgow, S.W.2.*

13

PERCHERONS. Native to the Perche Valley in Normandy, these medium weight draught horses probably have Arab origins. This is evident in the arched shape of the head and neck. They have good bone structure, a wide chest, short legs and large feet. They are very spirited horses and trot well which is uncommon. They are generally easy to handle. The absence of hair on their legs makes for easy grooming. The majority are grey or black in colour. The Breed Society is known as *The British Percheron Society, Owen Webb House, Gresham Road, Cambridge.*

SHIRES. The largest and heaviest of the draught horses, Shires are immensely strong and are predominant in most English horse shows. They are noted for being sweet tempered and easy to handle though they are somewhat slow moving. They were probably used in the Middle Ages by Knights wearing excessively heavy armour. Shires average about 17 hands and there are no really distinctive colours. One defect in the breed is the lengthy feather, which may be coarse. This is an indication of poor quality bone, but has largely been eradicated in modern Shires. The Breed Society is *The Shire Horse Society, 17 Devonshire Street, London W.1.*

15

SUFFOLK PUNCHES originated in East Anglia and are a very pure breed of horse. They are always chestnut in colour, clean legged, with small feet, a strong arched neck and small ears. They are fairly fast moving strong horses, with large bodies and short legs. They stand at about 16 hands. They have a remarkably long working life and work well on small quantities of poor quality feed. The Breed Society is *The Suffolk Horse, 6 Church Street, Woodbridge, Suffolk.*

Other Breeds of Horses are:—

ANGLO-ARAB. This is a composite breed generally derived from a Thoroughbred mare and an Arab horse. These are two very pure breeds of horses and for this reason it can take its place among the world's breeds of horses. The Anglo-Arab varies in height and can look almost pure Arab or pure Thoroughbred. It is an extremely intelligent spirited horse and often figures in point-to-points, steeplechasing, and show jumping. It can be used as a pack or a hunter. A stud book is maintained by *The Arab Horse Society (of England), Beechmead, Rowledge, Farnham, Surrey.*

17

ARAB, an absolutely pure species which ran wild in Arabia thousands of years ago. It has been used for centuries as a race horse in the Middle East, and the Arabs went to great pains to maintain the purity of its blood. Now nearly every breed and cross breed of horse has some Arab blood in its veins. It has passed on its qualities of stamina and strength though it has been surpassed in speed by the Thoroughbred which has Arab blood in it. Outstanding characteristics are the curved neck, high tail carriage, wide tapering head and small ears. It stands at about 14½ hands and can survive on a very frugal diet. The Breed Society is *The Arab Horse Society (of England), Beechmead, Rowledge, Farnham, Surrey.*

CLEVELAND BAY. A breed of English horse which is perhaps the oldest of its kind. It is indigenous to Yorkshire. It is useful for crossing with other breeds as it passes on many of its fine qualities such as its staying power and its good appearance to its offspring. Typical characteristics are its all over bay colour, the absence of hair on its fairly short legs, and a powerful body with strong quarters. It has been claimed that the Cleveland Bay will work as well as most heavy horses and at a greater speed. Cleveland Bays make useful carriage horses and are still predominant amongst the Carriage horses in the Royal Mews, which are used for ceremonial purposes. The famous show jumper "Foxhunter" had several strains of Cleveland Bay in his blood. The Breed Society is *The Cleveland Bay Horse Society, Midge Hall, Roxby, Staithes, Yorkshire.*

HACKNEY. A breed of pony or harness horse which has a long stride and high trotting action, which makes it appear to fly over the ground. It derives from the Norfolk Trotter which is itself a cross-bred horse, with some Arab blood in it. Years ago it was used for carrying large weights at high speeds; it is not a good saddle horse. A good Hackney is one of the most popular horses in the show ring. The legs when trotting should be kept true with no flaying of hooves; when standing still the legs should be straight covering the maximum amount of ground, and the whole attitude should be one of alertness. The Breed Society is *The Hackney Horse Society, 16 Bedford Square, London, W.C.1.*

HUNTER. This is not an actual breed of horse but a class or type used for hunting. The type of country in which the hunt takes place governs to some extent the characteristics of the horse. It should be courageous, responsive, a good jumper, holding its head well up. The show-hunter is of course the ideal and is virtually Thoroughbred. Show-hunters are divided into three classes according to weight. The market value increases in proportion to the weight that the horse can comfortably carry. The Breed Society is *The Hunters' Improvement and National Light Horse Breeding Society, 16 Devonshire Street, London, W.1.* They also maintain a Hunter Stud Book.

THOROUGHBRED. The Thoroughbred is capable of very high speeds and has become predominant as a race horse. It traces back to Arab stock, the three best known sires being Godolphin Arabian, Darley Arabian and Byerley Turk. The Thoroughbred has overcome the typical slowness of the Arab. It can be an extremely beautiful horse having a long graceful neck, a small head and a shapely body. However performance on the race-course counts far more than physical appearance. The breeding and Stud Book is controlled by *Messrs. Weatherby and Sons.*

YORKSHIRE COACH HORSE. A large, powerful horse much used for pulling elegant coaches and carriages. It originated in the East Riding of Yorkshire. It is difficult to distinguish it from the Cleveland Bay, though it is in fact a separate breed produced by cross breeding the Thoroughbred with the Cleveland Bay. The weight and size of this horse varies enormously though it is generally large and powerful up to 16.2 hands. It has a large, long body with muscular shoulders and fairly short legs: which make it suitable for road work. The breed is no longer popular since there is very little use for coaches these days. *The Yorkshire Coach Horse Society now amalgamated with The Cleveland Bay Horse Society.*

The Main Breeds of Ponies are:—

CONNEMARA. An ancient breed of ponies indigenous to Western Ireland, where until comparatively recently they ran wild. Controlled breeding has not decreased the good qualities of this hardy, docile animal. Its height limit is now 14.2 hands and it is generally grey in colour. The Breed Society is *The English Connemara Society, The Quinta, Bentley, Farnham, Surrey.*

DALES. This is a hardy breed of pony native to North Eastern England. It is extremely strong and rather stocky possibly owing to the introduction of some Clydesdale blood into the breed. It was originally used as a pack pony for carrying large quantities of lead from the mines in Northumberland and Durham to the docks. It has proved its ability to cope with the work of a small farm almost as effectively as a draught horse. The predominant colour is black. The Breed Society is *The Dales Pony Improvement Society, Hollin Hill Farm, Hamsterley, Bishop Auckland, Co. Durham.*

DARTMOOR. A breed of pony which has lived for centuries on Dartmoor. It has become well adapted to its environment and is therefore hardy and able to survive on a frugal diet. It is a friendly long lived pony and makes an excellent mount for children. The average height is 12.2 hands and there is no predominant colour. Some of the mares make excellent polo ponies. The Breed Society is *The Dartmoor Pony Society, Lower Hisley, Lustleigh, Newton Abbot, Devon.*

EXMOOR. A very old breed of pony indigenous to the wild moorland country of Somerset and Devon, probably descended from the British wild horse. It is a hardy pony of about 12.2, 12.3 hands, used to difficult conditions and a sparse diet. It makes a very good children's pony and has a short, springy coat either brown or bay in colour with no white, and a mealy nose or muzzle. The Breed Society is *The Exmoor Pony Society, Gapland Orchard, Hatch Beauchamp, Taunton, Somerset.*

FELL. There is very little to distinguish the breed from the Dales Pony, though it comes from the North West of England whereas the Dales comes from the North East. The Fell is slightly shorter and less stocky than the Dales, it is equally useful as a hard working, weight-carrying pony and it makes a very good mount. The usual colour is black or dark brown; mane, tail, and feather are thick and curly. The Breed Society is *The Fell Pony Society*, *Packway*, *Windermere*, *Westmorland*.

HIGHLAND. A fairly large thick-set breed, similar to a cob, mainly found in the Highlands of Scotland. Height varies from 12.2 to 14.2 hands according to type. It is sure footed and strong and has been used as a worker pony by glen farmers and crofters. One of its chief uses is as a mount for stalkers and as a riding pony. Crossing with Arabs and Clydesdales has increased the qualities of these ponies. Grey is the commonest colour though blacks and browns are quite usual. It has a graceful crested neck, strong shoulders, flat bones, legs and flowing tail and mane. The Breed Society is *The Highland Pony Society, 32 Rutland Square, Edinburgh.*

NEW FOREST. This breed is native to the New Forest in Hampshire. Next to the Highland it is the largest of the nine breeds of wild pony to be found in Britain. There has been some cross breeding among the ponies, Queen Victoria for instance loaned an Arab Stallion which was loosed in the New Forest for several years. It is a narrow pony, with a large head with some Arab characteristics. It is sure footed and fearless. Feed is very sparse, so the ponies are economical feeders and make very good family ponies, as they are very easy to break in. The Breed Society is *The New Forest Pony Breeding and Cattle Society, Deeracres, Lisle Court, Lymington, Hants.*

SHETLAND. This is the smallest of all breeds of pony and it originated in the Shetland Isles off the North of Scotland. In spite of its height it is an extremely strong pony and was widely used as a pit pony before the days of mechanisation in the mines. The average height of a Shetland is 9.3 hands, it is one of the hardiest of ponies being used to a frugal diet which in winter may consist solely of seaweed.

It is sure footed and has a very long, straight mane, and tail, and is generally black, brown or bay. It is a very docile pony and popular as a children's pony and a family pet. It is claimed that it is harmful to learn to ride on a Shetland pony. They have been exported all over the world. The Breed Society is *The Shetland Pony Stud Book Society, 61 George Street, Perth.*

WELSH PONY. Not to be confused with the Welsh Mountain Pony or the Welsh Cob, this pony has been bred from a combination of both, together with some Hackney blood. It is a ride and drive pony of good ability, standing at between 12.2 and 13.2 hands. The Breed Society is *The Welsh Pony and Cob Society, Queen's Road, Aberystwyth, Wales.*

WELSH COB. This is an established breed founded on the Welsh Mountain Pony, and was used many years ago to develop the Fell pony, and also the Hackney horse and pony. It is renowned as a trotting pony, and has many tractive uses for the small farms, being a willing, good tempered worker, capable of pulling heavy loads. It is used as a riding cob, for both old and young. It is courageous and a good jumper so it makes an excellent hunter. The best type of Welsh cob comes from Cardiganshire. The Breed Society is *The Welsh Pony and Cob Society, Queen's Road, Aberystwyth, Wales.*

WELSH MOUNTAIN PONY. Perhaps the most beautiful of British ponies, the Welsh Mountain pony has survived the hardships of life in the mountains of Wales for centuries. It can still be found there in a wild or semi-wild state. It is an intelligent, plucky animal with great stamina, capable of carrying heavy weights. It has had many successes in the show ring and is a great favourite as a children's mount. Greys, browns and chestnuts are the most common colours. The Breed Society is *The Welsh Pony and Cob Society, Queen's Road, Aberystwyth, Wales.*

D.R.—B

GLOSSARY OF TECHNICAL TERMS

Bang-tail. A tail with the hair squared off close to the dock.

Barrel. Description of that part of a horse's body which is beneath the ribs.

Calf-knee. Fore-legs which, when viewed from the side, are concave.

Coffin Head. A big ugly head.

Colt. A male horse under the age of four.

Conformation. General expression to denote the make and shape of a horse, whether it is good or bad as a whole.

Cowhocks. Hocks which are turned inwards at the points, a sign of weakness.

Deep through the girth. A horse that is well-ribbed-up.

Dishing. A faulty movement of the fore-feet being thrown in an outer circular movement.

Ewe neck. When the line of the neck is concave.

Feather. Hair on the heels, or varying density and coarseness.

Fiddle-head. A large, and ugly-shaped head.

Filly. A female horse under the age of four.

Flat-sided. When a horse's ribs are not rounded.

Foal. A colt or filly up to the age of 12 months, and referred to as a colt-foal or a filly-foal.

Frog. V-shaped cushion in the sole of all four feet, which acts as a shock absorber.

Glass, china or wall eye. A light blue eye with a lot of white showing.

Goose rump. Where from behind the saddle the line runs rather sharply downwards to the tail.

Hollow back. Where the natural concave line of the back is exaggerated.

Mare. The female equine animal.

Over at the knee. When the knees are bent forwards.

Over-bent. When a horse's head and neck are bent and the chin is tucked into the breast.

Parrot-mouth. A malformation of the upper jaw which hinders a horse from grazing.

Pin-toes. Toes which turn inwards.

Roach-back. A prominent convex spinal column.

Roman nose. A head with a convex face.

Short of a rib. Where there is a marked space between the last rib and the point of the hip.

Sickle Hocks. Hocks which have a sickle-like appearance when looked at from the side.

Stallion. A horse capable of reproducing himself, also known as "entire" or "whole horse".

Tied-in below the knee. Where the measurement immediately below the knee is considerably less than the measurement taken lower down the leg.

Well ribbed-up. Well sprung ribs providing heart and lung room.

Well-topped. A horse of good conformation above the legs.

Points of the Horse

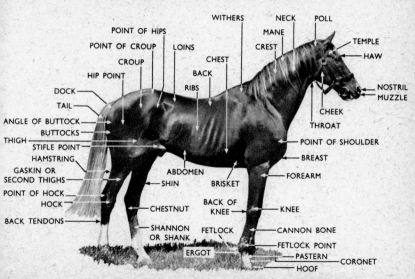

POINT OF HIPS · WITHERS · NECK · POLL · POINT OF CROUP · LOINS · MANE · CREST · TEMPLE · HAW · CROUP · CHEST · HIP POINT · BACK · DOCK · RIBS · NOSTRIL · MUZZLE · TAIL · CHEEK · THROAT · ANGLE OF BUTTOCK · BUTTOCKS · THIGH · STIFLE POINT · POINT OF SHOULDER · HAMSTRING · BREAST · GASKIN OR SECOND THIGHS · ABDOMEN · FOREARM · SHIN · BRISKET · POINT OF HOCK · HOCK · CHESTNUT · BACK OF KNEE · KNEE · BACK TENDONS · SHANNON OR SHANK · FETLOCK · CANNON BONE · ERGOT · FETLOCK POINT · PASTERN · CORONET · HOOF

35

Horse's Tack

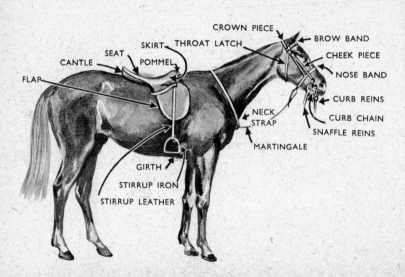

CROWN PIECE

THROAT LATCH

SKIRT

BROW BAND

SEAT

POMMEL

CHEEK PIECE

CANTLE

NOSE BAND

FLAP

CURB REINS

CURB CHAIN

NECK
STRAP

SNAFFLE REINS

MARTINGALE

GIRTH

STIRRUP IRON

STIRRUP LEATHER

CHAPTER THREE

Riding Equipment

The main items of equipment for riding consist of a saddle and a bridle. The saddle, on which the rider sits, goes on the horse's back; the bridle goes on the horse's head and is to assist the rider to control the horse.

SADDLE. The front is known as the *pommel*, the centre as the *seat* and the back as the *cantle*. The underneath is the lining and may be leather, linen or serge. Leather lasts longest and provided it is kept properly is very good. Linen lined saddles are easy to clean and to look after but don't last as long as leather lined ones. Serge does not wear well and is hard to keep clean. The sides of the saddle are called *saddle flaps* and underneath on each side is a *sweat flap* and *tabs* for the girth. At the top on each side of the saddle is a small metal bar known as the *stirrup bar* to carry the stirrup leathers. The *girth* is the fitting which keeps the saddle in place on the horse's back. Girths may be made of webbing, leather, string or nylon. Web girths do not wear well and are inclined to snap. Leather girths are good but must be kept clean and soft so that they do not gall the horse's flanks. String or nylon

| Saddle | Stirrups | Breastplate |

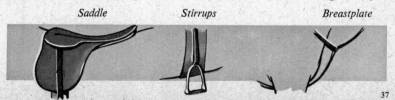

37

Page 38. (Left to right) **Bits**—*Snaffle, Pelham, Double.*

Page 39. (Left to right) **Bridles**—*Single, Double;*
Martingales—*Standing, Running, Irish.*

girths are good and easy to keep clean.

The *stirrup leathers* are the straps fitted through the stirrup bars on the saddle and carrying the stirrups. These should be of good strong leather as they are put to considerable strain. "Unbreakable" leathers can be obtained and, except that during the early part of their life they stretch rather easily, are probably the safest and best.

Stirrups, also known as *irons*, are the metal cups in which the rider's feet are placed. Stainless steel irons are expensive but are the best and safest. Nickel irons are not advisable as they are soft and inclined to bend.

BRIDLE. There are single and double bridles. The double bridle has a small snaffle as well as the curb bit in the horse's mouth and therefore needs two headpieces, one for the snaffle and the other for the bit. A single bridle has only one bit and therefore only one headpiece. Other parts of the bridle are *reins* for the rider to control the horse, *brow band* to keep the bridle in place on the horse's head, *noseband* which has its own headpiece and is for the fitting of a standing martingale if one is required, *throat lash* which is part of the headpiece and is to prevent the bridle being pulled over the horse's head. A *curb chain* is used with a

curb bridle and a *lip strap* is affixed to the curb chain to keep it in place.

BITS are the mouthpieces of the bridles and there are many varieties. Sufficient for the normal rider are : *snaffle* or *bridoon* which has a mouthpiece with rings at each end and no curb chain. *Pelham* which is a single curb bit with a curb chain and a *double* which consists of a small snaffle or bridoon and a curb bit with a curb chain.

MARTINGALES are used to control the position of the horse's head. There are three kinds: *Standing martingales* have one end attached to the girth and the other to the noseband. *Running martingales* have one end attached to the girth and the other end divides into two straps each with a ring on the end through which the reins are passed. *Irish martingales* consist of two rings connected by a strap about six inches long through which the reins pass and are used to keep the reins in place and stop them going over the horse's head.

BREASTPLATE consists of a leather neck strap attached to the front of the saddle on each side by short straps, and to the girth which passes through a loop and prevents the saddle from slipping back.

CHAPTER FOUR

Learning to Ride

It cannot be stressed too strongly that those wishing to learn to ride should take instruction from a reputable Riding School which employs Certificated Instructors. Whilst it may be possible to learn a lot from studying suitable text books, the novice's training will be speeded up tremendously under the eye of a good Instructor instead of arriving at the result by the "process of elimina-

The correct way to mount your horse.

The correct way to dismount your horse.

tion". The following is a very short guide on the subject.

MOUNTING. In order to ride, the rider must get on to the horse's back. Stand on the near (left-hand) side of the horse near the shoulder and facing slightly to the rear. Make sure the girths are tight. Hold the reins in the left hand just short enough to check the horse from moving. Using the right hand, place the left foot in the stirrup. Spring lightly up straightening the left leg and placing the right hand on the back of the saddle. Carry the right leg over the horse's back and sit quietly down in the saddle. Place the right foot in the off (right-hand) stirrup.

DISMOUNTING. Take both feet out of the stirrups. Place the left hand on the horse's neck and the right hand on the front (pommel) of the saddle. Vault off keeping the right leg clear of the horse's back and land lightly on both feet.

THE SEAT. The rider should sit well down in the centre of the saddle with the upper part of the body upright but not stiff, head erect and eyes looking to the front. Toes should be slightly up and heels down, this strengthens the grip. The inside of the knees and thigh should be against the saddle. If the toe is turned too far out the knee will be drawn away from the saddle. If turned in the position will become stiff and unnatural. The lower part of the leg should be kept back and away from the horse's sides. The stirrup leather should be perpendicular and, with the head erect, a glance downwards should show the toe of the boot or shoe just in front of the knee cap.

HOLDING THE REINS. Normally the reins should be held in both hands. The following may be found a satisfactory method:—With a single rein bridle, to hold the reins in both hands, first take the reins into the left hand with the right rein between the first and second fingers and the left rein outside the fourth finger. Then place the right hand on the right rein with the rein outside the little finger and take it from the left hand. The hands should be about 4 inches apart. With a double-rein bridle place the little finger of the left hand between the two left reins and the second finger between the two right reins, then place the little finger of the right hand between the two right reins and separate the two hands about 4 inches apart.

THE AIDS are the signals by means of which the rider conveys to the horse

The correct seat—you must sit well before you can ride well.

42

what he wants him to do. There are two types of "Aids". Natural and Artificial.

NATURAL AIDS consist of the legs which send the horse on and control the hindquarters, the hands which check or allow pace and control the front part of the horse, the voice which can encourage and quieten the horse.

ARTIFICIAL AIDS consist of whips, spurs, martingales etc., which may be used to reinforce the natural aids.

USE OF THE AIDS. To go forward or to increase the pace, close both legs to the horse and push him forward regulating the speed by pressure on the reins and decreasing the pressure of the legs.

To stop or to decrease the pace, close both legs with a squeezing pressure, increase the feeling on the reins until the required pace is obtained or the horse stops, then relax the pressure of the legs and the feeling on the reins.

To turn or circle to the right increase the pressure of the right rein and the left leg. To turn or circle to the left reverse these aids.

In order to ride, the rider must first get on to the horse's back!

43

GLOSSARY OF RIDING TERMS

Aids. The signals through which a rider conveys to the horse what he wishes him to do.

Balance. When a horse carries itself and the weight of the rider in such a way that it can use itself to the best advantage.

Behind the Bit. When a horse will not take hold of the bit.

Bolter. A horse that runs away with its rider.

Boring. When a horse leans on the bit and is on its forehand.

Breastplate. A leather device to prevent the saddle from slipping back.

Bridle. A leather headpiece to which the bits and reins are attached.

Canter. A slow gallop.

Cantle. Back part of the saddle.

Collection. Shortening the pace by pressure on the reins and increased pressure of the legs.

Curb-chain. A small chain fitted to some bits.

Forehand. The head, neck, shoulders, and forelegs of a horse.

Forging. The striking of the hind shoe against the fore shoe when the horse is trotting.

Gall. A sore place caused by badly fitted saddlery.

Gallop. A pace of four time—the fastest pace of a horse.

Girth. The strap which keeps the saddle in place.

Hack. A riding horse.

Hand. The measurement by which the height of a horse is recorded. A hand equals 4 inches.

Handiness. The ability of a horse to turn quickly and smoothly at the will of the rider.

Hogged Mane. Where the mane has been cut short.

Impulsion. A forward urge generated by the use of the hocks.

Independent Seat. When the rider has a firm seat and is independent of the reins.

Jibbing. When the horse refuses to move forward, and sometimes runs back. Also called "Napping".

Leg-up. Assistance given to a rider to mount.

Lip-strap. A thin leather strap which prevents the curb-chain from riding up.

Martingale. A strap to control the position of the horse's head.

Nappy. A horse that resists its rider. See "Jibbing".

Near-side. The left side when viewed from the rear.

Noseband. A broad leather band worn between the cheeks and the bit.

Noseband, Dropped. Attached round the muzzle below the bit.

Numnah. A felt, rubber or sheepskin pad worn beneath the saddle.

Off-side. The right side when viewed from the rear.

On the bit. When a horse takes a definite feel on the reins.

One-sided Mouth. A mouth which is unresponsive on one side.

Over-bent. When a horse's head and neck are bent and the chin is tucked into the breast.

Pelham. A form of single curb bit used universally for polo.

Plate. A light shoe for racing.

Pommel. The front arch of the saddle.

Rein back. When the horse steps backwards.

Saddle. A leather padded seat which goes on the horse's back and on which the rider sits.

Saddle Bars. Metal fittings on the saddle to which the stirrup leathers are attached.

Saddle-flaps. Leather sides of a saddle.

Saddle-tree. The frame on which the saddle is made.

Seat. The position of the rider in the saddle.

Snaffle Bridle. A bridle with a snaffle bit.

Sound. A horse free from any form of defect or lameness.

Spurs. An artificial aid worn on the rider's boots.

Star Gazer. A horse which carries its head too high.

Stirrup Iron. A metal fitting into which the rider's foot is placed.

Tack. A stable word for Saddlery or Harness.

Throat Lash or Latch. A narrow strap which goes under the throat and prevents the bridle from being pulled over the horse's head.

Trot. A pace of two time in which diagonal pairs of legs touch the ground together.

Trot, Rising at. The rider rises in the saddle at one stride, misses the next and comes down again.

Walk. A pace of four time.

CHAPTER FIVE

Show Jumping

In the early days, whether in battles or sport, it was not necessary for the horse to jump except perhaps occasionally a ditch or small bank. However in the eighteenth century, with the passing of the Enclosure Act, things changed considerably, and no longer was it possible to gallop across country without jumping, and it was not long before people began to realise not only that the horse was a natural jumper but also that there was a tremendous thrill in this new form of horsemanship.

The first mention of Show Jumping competitions being held was at a harness horse show in Paris in 1866 when a class for Show Jumpers was included. The competitors appeared in the ring to parade before the spectators and were then sent out into the nearby country to jump some natural obstacles. This was obviously not very interesting to the spectator, and so after a short period it was so organised that a few fences were built in the arena. In 1900 the sport came to England and was known as "leaping", and even today shows in various parts of the country advertise their jumping competitions as "leaping competitions". The sport was very slow to appeal to competitors in this country and often classes only had fifteen to twenty entries, and it was a common sight to see ladies riding side-saddle.

In 1912, Show Jumping received its first major recognition when Equestrian Events were included in the Olympic Games for the first time; however only men were allowed to compete, and this is a rule that was only relaxed by the Olympic Committee in 1956, and the first lady to compete in Olympic Show Jumping was Miss Pat Smythe riding Mr. R. Hanson's Flanagan.

When the sport was first included in the Olympic Games there were no general rules, for each country had its own which varied tremendously, and so the Fédération Equestre Internationale was formed to standardise the rules.

In Britain there were no standard rules for judging competitions and each show decided how the judging should be conducted. The chief judge was generally the local Master of Foxhounds who was assisted by a prominent member of the Hunt, with an equally vague, though not unprejudiced, mind, and so the competition would probably be won by some good hunting friend. All of this caused immense dissatisfaction among competitors. A typical course consisted of gorsed hurdles and some thin larch poles, and if the show was particularly enterprising it would include a water jump, though usually when it came to the turn for the jumping competition the water had evaporated from the jump or seeped away.

Left—Col. M. P. Ansell, C.B.E., D.S.O., Chairman of the British Show Jumping Association since 1945, with Col. Talbot Ponsonby.

47

As there were no rules for judging, the judges made up their own, and some gave marks according to the severity of the jump, whilst others gave marks for the style of the rider, and if a competitor had three refusals at a fence he was usually asked to go on and try the next fence. It was, indeed, quite a usual thing to show the horse the fence before jumping it.

The most severe type of fence that was met, was a single pole which had no ground line and sometimes in a jump-off would reach a height of 5 feet. Although this caused quite a lot of amusement to the crowd, as often, when the pole reached this height, small horses used to duck their heads and dive underneath, it was very dangerous to the rider.

Therefore with all this variance in the judging and the competitions it was obvious something had to be done, and the British Show Jumping Association was formed. The jumping competitors, both serving officers and civilians, decided that it was necessary to have an association to protect them from the whims of judges and executives. A meeting was held at Olympia in 1923, when the British Show Jumping Association was formed, and finally it was incorporated under the Companies Act on the 31st December 1925. The main object of the Association ever since it was formed has been "The encouragement of show jumping", and it is concerned with Show Jumping and Show Jumping only. The newly formed Association immediately set itself to the introduction of a code of rules for the sport. In the first place these were based mainly on the existing international rules, little known in England at that time. Not unnaturally as a result of past experience the emphasis of all new rules was on what jumps might or might not be used, and the Association sought to protect its members, not only by the introduction of rules for judging and a list of approved judges, but by laying down restrictions on courses and obstacles. The sincere efforts made by the early committees formed a sound foundation for the present Association which now has 3,244 Jumping members, 938 Non-jumpers, 444 Associates and 1,623 Junior members as well as 1,040 Affiliated shows. The present Chairman of

A general view of White City Stadium showing the lay-out of jumps for the Royal International Horse Show.

the Association is Colonel M. P. Ansell, C.B.E., D.S.O.—a position he has held since 1945—and during its history the Association has been well served by many people, but no one man has done so much for Show Jumping as Mike Ansell.

Registration and grading were introduced and a headquarters started in Sloane Street in 1945 to deal with the increasing amount of recording work which these innovations brought with them. Another good "fillip" to equestrianism as a whole after the war, was the fact that the Olympic Games were held at Wembley, and it was soon realised that if Great Britain were to act as the host nation they must be well represented at Show Jumping, just as much as at any other sport, and as a result it was a just reward and great achievement that the team consisting of Lt. Col. Llewellyn on Foxhunter, Lt. Col. Nichol on Kilgeddin and Major Carr on Monty won Bronze medals. The years between 1948 and 1952 were years of triumph for show jumping, as this rather new sport was immensely popular with the public.

Finally the winning of the Gold Medals at Helsinki thrilled the whole country and show jumping was on the map.

Almost every horse show now stages jumping competitions as part of their main ring attractions, and many show Societies have considered that a good jumping competition is more of an attraction than paying for some expensive display. The two main shows are the Royal International Horse Show which is held at the White City in London in July and the Horse of the Year Show at the Empire Pool, Wembley in October. Both these shows are immensely popular with the public, and at the Horse of the Year Show, the "House Full" notices have to be put out nearly every night. Show jumping is a great sport today and provided it continues to be conducted on the right lines its future is assured. The international effort must be maintained as there can be little doubt that it is this which has provided the chief stimulus.

CHAPTER SIX

Show Jumping Courses and Obstacles

A jumping competition is decided on the way the horse jumps the fences, therefore the chief consideration must always be the layout of the course and the building of the obstacles. It must always be remembered that the intention of the course builder is to promote good natural jumping. Although the fences may be big they should encourage the horse and rider to meet them with confidence. Generally the course varies in length from between 500 yards to 900 yards, and will include ten to sixteen obstacles. The fences should be strong and solid in appearance.

OBSTACLES.

Each obstacle requires the horse to make one single jump or effort, and whilst obstacles should be varied they may be divided into two categories:—

(a) The straight obstacle, this is so built that all the elements of which it is built are in the same vertical plane to the ground. Examples are, gates, walls, posts and rails, and planks. A single rail at 4′ 3″ will be a difficult obstacle, but with more rails added underneath, it has a more solid appearance and becomes easier to jump. Narrow fences such as the stile and the small gate are a test of obedience of the horse.

(b) The spread fence, this is so built that it necessitates the horse jumping width as well as height. Examples are, Triple Bars, Double Oxer, Hog's Back, parallel bars, and water. A triple bar with a spread of six or seven feet and a height of 4′ 9″ will be a comparatively easy obstacle compared with parallel bars standing at 4′ 6″ with a six foot spread.

The water jump will vary in width between 12 and 16 feet overall, this includes a small brush obstacle on the take-off side about 2 feet high.

THE GROUND LINE.

The horse when approaching a fence judges the point at which it intends to take off by looking at the line at the base of the fence, this is known as the Ground Line. In order to jump successfully a horse must take off at the correct place. A fence such as the water which rests on the ground has a distinct ground line. A single rail makes a difficult fence, as it has no ground line. A fence is made easier by bringing the ground line slightly on to the approach side of the obstacle.

Obstacles should always be as wide as possible, and never less than 11 feet; remember, the greater the height, the greater should be the width. Certain component parts such as wings, poles and stands are common to all obstacles, but with the aid of bush fences, gates, and walls, a great variety may be introduced.

When deciding the heights of obstacles there are four points to take into account:

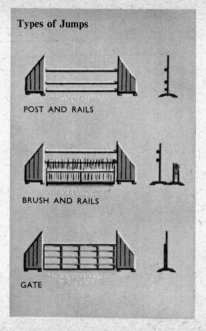

Types of Jumps

POST AND RAILS

BRUSH AND RAILS

GATE

(a) the condition of the ground.

(b) the position of the obstacle in the course. If early in the course it should be smaller than if it is later when the horses are in their stride.

(c) the setting of the fence; if it is placed immediately after a sharp turn, or the background makes it difficult to see it should be small.

(d) the nature of the obstacle and the material with which it is made; a solid and well made obstacle can be built larger than a flimsy one.

COMBINATION OBSTACLES.

When the material for the building of a Show Jumping Course is limited, in order to obtain a decisive result there is a danger of the dimensions of the obstacles becoming too great, with the result that an Open Class develops into a Test or Puissance Event. If a study is made of the distances between obstacles in relation to the problems which variations in such distances pose to horse and rider, this danger can be avoided. This is particularly applicable to Combination Obstacles. Doubles and trebles are obstacles which can set various tests of the

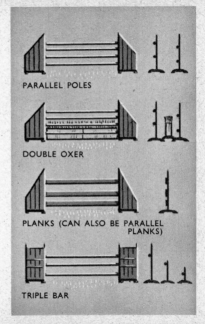

PARALLEL POLES

DOUBLE OXER

PLANKS (CAN ALSO BE PARALLEL PLANKS)

TRIPLE BAR

Types of Jumps

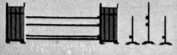

HOGS BACK

REVERSED OXER

SMALL WALL AND RAILS

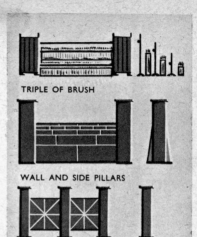

TRIPLE OF BRUSH

WALL AND SIDE PILLARS

HELSINKI GATES

SMALL WALL, BRUSH AND RAILS

54

ability of horse and rider. The distances between the fences comprising these obstacles are the means whereby the course-builder can provide different tests or problems. Thus, a distance which proves to be shorter than that suitable to a normal horse's stride will test the horse's obedience to the rider's hand and leg, whilst one that is wider will demand the maintenance and production of impulsion. When laying out such obstacles with wide distances, the course-builder must ensure that the first obstacle is of solid structure, and of a type to encourage bold and free jumping. Distances in combination obstacles are measured from centre to centre of each fence comprising the obstacle. The distance between any two of the obstacles must be not less than 24 feet and not more than 39 feet 4 inches.

JUMPING COURSES.

On pages 56 to 65 will be found eight course plans, which are given as a guide. It will be noticed how from each set of plans different competitions can be given a change of course by moving only the minimum number of obstacles. The distance between the main obstacles should be thirty yards or multiples of three yards, but the distances must be measured on a track which would be taken by an experienced and careful rider.

All courses except sometimes in speed classes should flow smoothly and have no sharp turns and nothing be included that might be a trap, but at least one or preferably two changes of direction should be given. Generally speaking, it is good policy to alternate straight and spread obstacles as far as possible over the whole course.

It is important when designing a course to remember three main points:—

(i) The obstacles should encourage the horse to jump.

(ii) Test the horse's ability to jump.

(iii) Provide entertainment for the spectators.

Thus, the first one or two obstacles should be inviting and the bigger and more spectacular obstacles should be in the most prominent positions and usually are better jumped when the horses are going towards the collecting ring. The course should be designed so

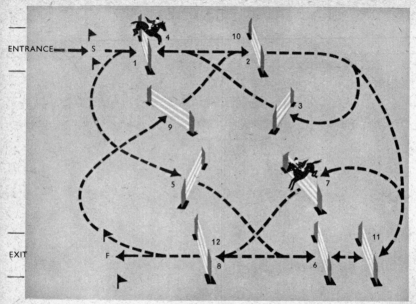

Competition—Open

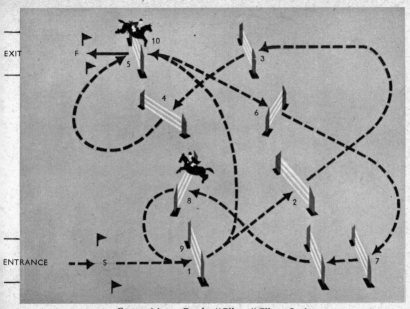

EXIT

ENTRANCE

Competition—Grades "B" or "C" or Junior

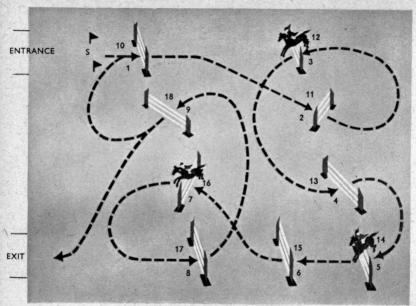

Competition—Hit and Hurry

ENTRANCE

EXIT

Competition—Take your own Line

that the obstacles are never in a line across the ring. A full day should be allowed for designing and building a course.

The following are suggestions for improving obstacles:—

Straw Bales.

(a) Use under poles to fill in open spaces, e.g. under the front rail of a hog's back or both rails of Parallel Poles.

(b) As a bank just in front of Post and Rails, this is particularly useful if the obstacle is to be jumped in both directions, for it will be easy one way and more difficult the other way.

(c) With hedge trimmings pushed between the straw and the string it makes a very effective bush fence.

(d) As padding to wings, to block in the sides of the obstacle.

(e) Built to form a broken wall with rails behind.

All the above may be covered with grass matting as a good variation from the natural colour, this may usually be acquired from the local greengrocer.

Hedge Trimmings and Shrubs.

(a) May be used as wings, if bundled together and then dropped over a stake driven into the ground.

(b) To decorate fences, inserted into the ground in front of poles and gates.

(c) To make bush fences.

(d) Bundled together and tied as faggots to go in front of or under poles, or as the take-off fence to a water jump.

Sacks.

Stuffed with straw and used in conjunction with wings and rustic fences, make a very good padding.

Oil Drums and Milk Churns.

These may be used as an alternative to straw bales, they should always be used on their sides, as they may prove dangerous if they stand upright.

Hurdles.

(a) They make a good filling if used under obstacles.

(b) Used either horizontally or vertically and tied to fencing posts, they make good wings, particularly for rustic obstacles.

Natural Obstacles.

(a) Small water or ditches. These should be about six inches deep, and four feet wide, and may be used with poles or brush in front, behind or in the centre.

(b) *Tree Trunks*—with poles over, make an excellent solid type rustic obstacle.

Flowers and Shrubs.

Used in conjunction with obstacles or wings, these are an ideal form of decoration.

Water Jump.

The most practical form should be from 10 to 12 ft. wide, and constructed so as to be jumpable from both sides, and from 12 ft. to 14 ft. across. It should be sloped from either direction with a maximum depth of water at the centre of 6 inches. The width of 10 ft. will enable it to be used for novice and junior competitions, and when used for bigger classes, the fence or poles on the take-off edge may be drawn forward, thus increasing the spread as required.

A level site extending either side of the jump should be chosen, and great care should be exercised in removing the turf from the area of the jump, so that after the show the hole may be filled in with soil and consolidated, the turf may then be relaid well stamped down and fine soil brushed into the joints.

There are various ways of sealing the bottom of the jump to retain the water, the most usual being "puddled clay" to a thickness of 3 inches. If this method is used allowance must be made for this depth when digging the hole. Another method is coconut matting or rubber, laid on a tarpaulin base; in this method care should be taken to ensure that they are taken on at least one foot on the take-off and landing sides, and flush with the surrounding ground, and firmly secured with pegs to make certain there is no danger of slipping and no edges protruding.

A bush fence or similar should always be placed on the take-off side and constructed to slope towards the water at an angle of 25-30 degrees, and approximately 2 ft. to 2 ft. 6 inches high. As much blanking out of the sides and edges as possible should be done, by use of wing stands, shrubs and flowers, thus making the jump attractive and encouraging the horse to the centre of the obstacle.

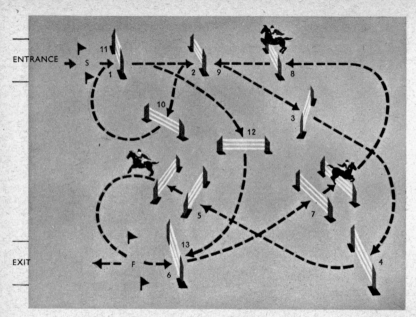

Competition—Open

62

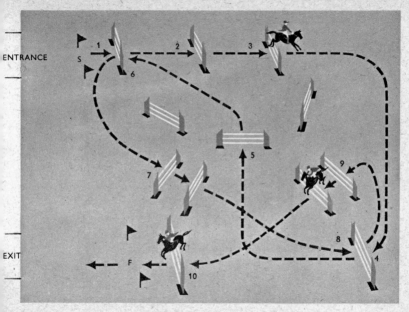

ENTRANCE

EXIT

Competition—Grades "B" or "C"

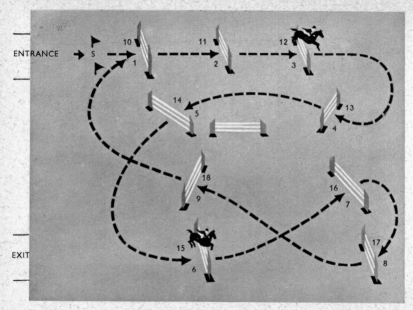

ENTRANCE →

EXIT

Competition—Hit and Hurry

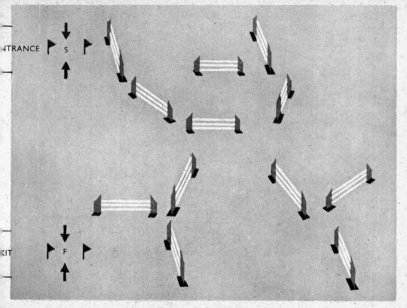

Competition—Take your own Line

CHAPTER SEVEN

The Main Horse Shows

In the United Kingdom the show jumping season begins at the end of March and continues until October, and it is proposed to deal with this section in two parts:

(a) International and (b) National.

INTERNATIONAL

The regulations governing International Horse Shows throughout the world are the responsibility of the Fédération Equestre Internationale (F.E.I.), and the calendar of these shows is prepared by the F.E.I. when it meets in December of each year. No official international event may take place unless it has been entered in the calendar of the F.E.I., and once a show has been arranged the locality and the date may not be changed without the authority of the F.E.I.

An official International Event may only be held in a country whose National Federation is a member of the F.E.I. and only the riders of such countries may be invited to take part.

In Europe only one official event of the same category, i.e. dressage, combined training or show jumping, may be held in each country. Outside Europe two official events of the same category may be organised in each country, though they may not both be held in the same town.

The rules and the schedule of each official International Event must be submitted in either French or English to the Secretary of the F.E.I. prior to the event so that he may check the schedule to ensure that they comply with the Regulations.

The only people eligible to compete in an official Event are (a) Amateur Riders who are nationals of the country

Ladies' class lines up for the presentation of awards at the Royal Windsor Horse Show.

where the Show is held, either by invitation or as indicated by the schedule and (b) Amateur Riders from foreign countries either officially invited or by personal invitation through their National Federation. Shows wishing to include Professional Riders may do so in a percentage of the Competitions on application to the F.E.I.

The organising committee of an official international event are responsible for the living expenses of the judges, the team captains, the members of official teams, their horses and grooms, (this is usually based on one groom to two horses) and also for the travelling expenses of the horses belonging to the official teams and of their grooms from the frontiers of the country where the show is being held to the place of the event and similarly on the return journey. These expenses may also be offered either wholly or in part to individual riders taking part who are not members of an official team representing their country.

The importance of the international effort of any National Federation cannot be over-emphasised, for so long as a N.F. has a strong international team backed with good reserves it will thrive. Any sport must depend upon its power to draw and interest spectators, and particularly in Show Jumping the great value to the spectator is that the riders of a particular country can ride against those of other countries abroad and beat them. Colonel Mike Ansell once said "You must have Stars, not Satellites and these are made abroad, not at home."

NATIONAL

The heading "Horse Shows" in this country covers a vast field of events from small village gymkhanas to shows such as the Royal International. In addition there are many Agricultural and Horticultural shows which include Horse and Pony Classes and Jumping events.

The small shows probably only have five or six gymkhana events for the local children, and these may consist of bending races, musical chairs, potato-picking and such events. Then the larger shows may include specialised sections, such as hunter classes, pony classes, breeding classes and jumping competitions.

It is impossible to determine how many shows are held in England during a year, but a guide is given by the fact that any show which holds show jumping competitions and where any prize exceeds £3, has to be affiliated to the British Show Jumping Association, and during 1960 there were 1,040 shows affiliated—of course, in addition to these all the Breed Societies hold their own specialised shows, and in the same way that shows holding jumping classes have to be affiliated to the B.S.J.A., so shows holding particular breed classes have to be affiliated to that particular Breed Society. Each breed society draws

A lighthearted race often seen at gymkhanas—"The Laundry Stakes".

up its own rules and conditions and also selects its panel of judges who again are experts at their job. All judges act in a voluntary capacity, though it is the custom for the show to offer them their travelling and out of pocket expenses.

It is as well at this stage to consider something of the organisation of a show:—

1. Select a suitable date and when doing this it is advisable to find out the dates of other local functions so that your show does not clash with it. If you are expecting to receive entries from leading competitors, particularly in the jumping events, make sure that you do not clash with a major event where these people are likely to be.

2. Decide what sort of a show you want to have, but remember that the spectator likes variety, and continuous judging of any particular class or section becomes very boring. Any breed or society will advise you which are the best classes to hold for your particular area.

3. Decide how much prize money you are able to offer, remembering in particular that if you want the best competitors, you must give attractive prize money. A recommended ratio of entry fee to prize money for jumping competitions is 6d. in the £ of the total prize money for the class, for instance for a 20/- entry fee one would give £40 in prizes. This would be considerably increased at the bigger Shows.

4. Prepare a draft schedule, and before having it printed send details of their sections to the various breed societies, so that you ensure the correct wording

is printed, and at the same time, send the affiliation fee to the Society. For instance, the affiliation fee to the British Show Jumping Association is £3.10.0 for each day of a show. The advantages of affiliation are that the jumping classes may be held under B.S.J.A. rules which are copyright and may not be used at any show which is not affiliated and further, no member of the B.S.J.A. may compete at a show which is not affiliated if any prize in a jumping competition exceeds £3. Included in the affiliation fee is a Third Party and Public Liability Insurance for all sections of the show including food poisoning up to a maximum of £10,000 for any one accident. Voluntary and unpaid workers are also covered. A copy of the current rule book containing all the information required in connection with the running of jumping competitions and a copy of the "Suggestions for the Organisation of Jumping Competitions", which includes the correct wording for jumping competitions, an up-to-date Panel of B.S.J.A. judges and course-builders is sent. A number of sets of jumps and also of automatic timing equipment are available for hire at very inexpensive rates. Special judging cards are provided free of charge, and a special rosette is presented to the winner of each jumping competition.

5. It is always advisable to try to include a provisional Time Table in the schedule, so that when competitors make their entries they know at approximately what time they will be wanted in the ring. Having worked this out you will know how many entries you may take in each competition, therefore you should have a closing date for entries prior to the show, and when you have received sufficient entries do not accept any more, for the worst mistake a show organiser can make is a programme which runs late.

6. Having decided on the distribution of the schedules and having posted them, the next thing is to order the necessary judging books, numbers, competitors' and grooms' badges and rosettes, and when ordering rosettes remember to order more than you actually require, especially in the lower awards where one is likely to have a lot of division of prizes in Jumping Competitions. Chil-

dren take a great pride in winning a rosette, and therefore these should be as good as you can afford. The various breed societies to which the show is affiliated will be willing to offer their rosettes to the winners of certain classes, but these should be given in addition to the show's rosette.

7. The selection of judges is most important as many people will only show their animals under competent judges, and therefore the names of the judges should be given in the schedule, wherever possible. A show secretary should always be prepared to pay the travelling and out of pocket expenses of any judges. Remember that judging is an arduous task, and if you have a lot of classes, especially of jumping, you should have plenty of judges.

8. Publicity plays a very important part in whether a show is successful or not, and for the smaller show it may be divided into two phases, (a) approximately 2-3 weeks before the closing of entries, when advertisements should be put in the local press and "horsey" newspapers in order to attract would-be competitors, and (b) approximately 1-2 weeks before the Show, advertisements should appear in the local press in order to attract the public.

9. After the show the prize money should be paid out as soon as possible to the prize winners, and the necessary results sent immediately to the appropriate breed-societies and associations, so that their records may be kept up to date.

At the Show it is necessary to have good and efficient stewards and officials in order to ensure the smooth running of the show, and some of the more important ones are listed below:—

(a) The Show Director, who is very often the Chairman of the organising body, and will be responsible for all the arrangements on the ground and for co-ordinating the arrangements between the various sections of the Show.

(b) The Chief Ring Steward is responsible for all the events in the ring and for keeping the Show running to time. He should always ensure that the ring is never empty, for the public do not like paying to gaze into space.

(c) Each Section should have its own Chief Steward, who is responsible for warning all competitors when they are required in the main ring, and for seeing that they are there on time.

(d) The Chief Collecting Ring Steward is responsible for sending the Classes and Competitors into the ring, on this hinges much of the success of the Show, for it is here that valuable minutes can be gained or lost. He is also responsible to see that Competitors comply with any dress regulations that may be in force.

(e) The course-builder is responsible for erecting the jumping courses, and it should be remembered that if good jumping is required one must have good courses. If the services of a professional course-builder are required application should be made to the B.S.J.A.

(f) Arena Party, these are the people who are responsible for putting up the fences when they are knocked down, and there should be at least twelve of them. Service Personnel are excellent for this, however if they are not available the local Boy Scouts or Young Farmers are also very good, but this should be their only job on the day, as it is tiring work and often lasts for long hours.

(g) The Announcer is the most important person from the Spectators' point of view. He should make the show as interesting as possible, and if there are well known competitors he should say something of their past successes, and describe how the various classes are being judged and what the judges are looking for.

(h) Medical officer and Veterinary officers. The show organisers should ensure that there is always one representative of each of these professions present during the hours of the show.

(i) An important person often overlooked is a Clerk-of-the-Scales who is necessary for the jumping competitions if the value of the first prize is £50 or over, or if the class is a B.S.J.A. Adult Championship.

CHAPTER EIGHT

B.S.J.A. Rules and Regulations

All Shows which hold jumping competitions and where the prize money in any competition thereat exceeds £3 (Three pounds), must affiliate to the British Show Jumping Association, this affiliation costs £3.10.0 for each day of the Show, and the advantages of affiliation are dealt with in the Section entitled "The Main Horse Shows".

In order to compete at these Shows a person must be a Life member at £26.5.0, a Jumping or a Visiting member at an annual subscription of £2, an Associate member at an annual subscription of £1, that is a young person between the ages of 16 and 18, or a Junior member at an annual subscription of 10/-, that is any person under 16 years of age. The effective date for age limits is taken from the 1st January of each year, and not the date of birth or the date of the Show.

At all shows it is necessary for both the owner and rider to be jumping members or, where appropriate, associate or junior members.

It is also possible for supporters of Show Jumping to become Non-Jumping members of the Association at an annual subscription of £1.

It is not possible for a Junior to compete in Adult competitions except in a Local Competition restricted to a 15-mile radius, and the conditions allow for Adults and Juniors. However, a Junior may apply to transfer to the Adult Section for the season if he/she so wishes, but in this case he/she must remain in the Adult Section for the rest of the Season, and may not revert to the Junior Section until the following Season.

All horses and ponies competing at affiliated shows must be registered with the Association. The initial registration of a horse costs £1, and the annual re-registration fee is 10/-. The initial registration of a pony costs 10/- and the annual re-registration fee is 5/-. If a horse/pony is transferred from one member to another, a transfer fee of 10/- has to be paid, and the transfer may not be completed until the Secretary General has received a form signed by both parties agreeing to the transfer.

It is possible for members to lease a horse from one another provided the appropriate form is completed and that the period is for not less than 3 months.

Horses and ponies have to be entered in jumping competitions under their registered name, and the changing of names is not encouraged, but it may be done at a charge of £5. A pony must not exceed 14.2 h.h., measured without shoes. No pony may compete in Adult classes unless it has been registered as a horse and then it must remain in Adult classes for the remainder of the Season and may not compete in Junior classes until the following Season. Horses and ponies may only compete in the same class, if the radius does not exceed 15 miles and the conditions of the class allow it.

All horses and ponies are graded on cash winnings at affiliated shows, the details are as follows:—

From nil to under £100	*Grade 'C'*
From £100 to under £200	*Grade 'B'*
From £200 upwards	*Grade 'A'*

Ponies—

From nil to under £50	*Grade 'J.C.'*
From £50 upwards	*Grade 'J.A.'*

In the case of Horses/ponies imported from overseas, winnings substantiated by the National Federation or other competent authority must be declared at the time of registering. If the system of grading is based on other than cash winnings, the Secretary General assesses the figure from information received, but this will never be less than £30—except in the case of a horse which has no registered winnings at all. Any horse which has been selected to represent its country at a C.H.I.O. will be automatically graded 'A'.

Once a horse has been up-graded it may never, under any circumstances, be down-graded.

All jumping competitions at affiliated

shows are adjudicated under the Rules and Regulations of the B.S.J.A. If a show executive wishes to hold competitions under Fédération Equestre Internationale Rules application may be made to the B.S.J.A.

The B.S.J.A. present a special rosette to the winners of all jumping competitions, and the winner of a Junior competition may win a medal, for which application has to be made to the B.S.J.A., but no Pony may win more than one Medal in a season.

Competing in the Junior Jumping Class.

No minimum heights are laid down for obstacles, but there are maximum heights for certain competitions, these are as follows:—

Grade 'A', Grades A and B or Adult Open when the first prize is value £20 or less	4' 6"
Grade B	4' 6"
Grades B and C	4' 3"
Grade C	4' 0"
Grade JA Ponies	4' 3"
Grade JC Ponies	3' 9"

These heights only apply to first rounds, and may be exceeded in a Jump-off, though in Junior competitions the maximum height may never exceed 5 ft.

Combination obstacles are a combination of two or more obstacles and the distance between any two of these must not be less than 24 ft. nor more than 39 ft. 4 inches measured centre to centre. Water jumps are encouraged wherever possible, and in order to assist the B.S.J.A. now provides portable types. In Junior competitions the spread must not exceed 12 feet, and there must be a lath or tape on the landing side on the edge of the water.

The Judges are responsible for seeing

that the course complies with the Regulations before a competition starts, and they are also responsible for seeing that no dangerous obstacle has been included and that the course has been properly measured. This is important as a Time Allowed is fixed for all competitions. Under B.S.J.A. rules the speed is based on 300 yards per minute, and for every second or part of a second over this Time Allowed he is penalised $\frac{1}{4}$ fault. The Time Limit is double the Time Allowed and exceeding this entails elimination.

The order of jumping does not matter except in speed competitions, when, as it is an advantage to go late in the competition, the order has to be drawn and this is the responsibility of the Judges.

Whilst it is the duty of the Judges to endeavour to obtain a winner of every competition and the course should be set with this end in mind, the rules do not permit the holding of more than two jumps-off. When a jump-off is held it has to be over at least six obstacles, and if a combination obstacle or a water jump were included in the original course they have to be included in the jump-off.

Table of Common Faults:

Obstacle knocked down	*4 faults*
Horse/pony and/or Rider falls	*8 faults*
1st Refusal or resistance in the round	*3 faults*
2nd Refusal or resistance in the round	*6 faults*
3rd Refusal or resistance in the round	*Elimination*
Exceeding the Time Allowed	$\frac{1}{4}$ *fault for every second*
Exceeding the Time Limit	*Elimination*

There are 19 common ways in which a competitor may be eliminated:—

1. Starting before the start signal.
2. Jumping an obstacle before the start signal.
3. Failing to pass through the Start, within 60 seconds of the signal to start.
4. A third refusal, resistance etc., during a round.
5. Napping or refusing at an obstacle for more than 60 seconds.
6. Horse or rider leaving the ring.

7. Showing an obstacle to the horse.
8. Jumping or attempting to jump an obstacle in the wrong order.
9. Taking the wrong course.
10. Failing to jump or attempt to jump an obstacle included for timing.
11. Jumping an obstacle knocked over before it is reset or the signal given.
12. Unauthorised assistance.
13. Underweight on weighing in. (A minimum weight of 10 st. 7 lbs. has to be carried in all B.S.J.A. Championships, and when the first prize exceeds £50).
14. Failing to retake all the obstacles of a combination after a refusal etc.
15. After a fall, failing to re-take course from a point not nearer the finish.
16. Not crossing the finishing line mounted.
17. Failing to comply with Judges' orders.
18. Exceeding the time limit.
19. Entering or leaving the ring dismounted without permission. A circle, turn round, run out or resistance counts as a refusal for scoring purposes.

Definition of a run out. If a horse or pony, not being properly under control, avoids the obstacle, or jumps the obstacle outside the boundary flags or jumps the wing.

Definition of a resistance. If a horse or pony, wherever he may be, refuses to go forward, stops, runs back, rears etc., it shall be assumed a resistance.

Definition of a refusal. If a horse or pony stops in front of or passes an obstacle to be jumped, whether or not it knocks it down or displaces it.

Stopping in front of an obstacle without knocking it down, and without reining back followed immediately by a standing jump is not penalised.

After being eliminated a competitor may make up to two attempts to jump any other obstacle in the ring.

All faults, including refusals, at each obstacle during the various attempts will be totalled up at the end of the round.

Faults for a fall are in addition to any other faults made. A horse is considered to have fallen when the shoulder and quarters on the same side touch the ground or touch the obstacle and ground. A rider is considered to have fallen when there is a separation between him and his horse which necessitates his remounting or vaulting into the saddle.

Timing must be adopted where possible, whether this is stated in the schedule or not, but the operation of the Time element is the responsibility of the Judge, and unless he is satisfied that it can be implemented and operated fairly it should not be used.

The Time Allowed will be decided by the Judge and will be worked out on a basis of 300 yards per minute, according to the length of the course. Time may never be used to decide the result of a competition, except in the case of special competitions with their own rules.

The affairs of the B.S.J.A. are dealt with by the Executive Committee, which consists of 8 nationally elected members, 10 regionally elected members, 2 members nominated by the Scottish Branch, and not more than 2 co-opted members. This committee is elected by the Adult and Show members of the Association. This Committee elects from its members three Standing Committees. They are, the Standing Committee for Rules, the Standing Committee for International Affairs, and the Standing Committee for Finance.

Scotland is administered as a Branch of the Association and England and Wales are divided into Areas. The Executive Committee appoint a Representative for each Area to look after the affairs of the Association. They are appointed at the first meeting of the Executive Committee after the Annual General Meeting in each year, to serve for twelve months.

The permanent Staff of the Association, appointed by the Executive Committee consists of:—

(a) **at the Headquarters in London:**
    The Secretary General.
    The Deputy Secretary General.
    The Public Relations Officer.
    A secretarial Staff of approximately 12.
(b) **at the Jump Store at Aldershot.**
    The Store Manager.
    The Assistant Store Manager.

During the show season, the Store Manager and his assistant both work as course-builders.

CHAPTER NINE

Some Well Known Show Jumpers

AHERLOW. Brown Mare owned by E. Holland-Martin and ridden by Owner, Lt. Col. D. N. Stewart and Lt. Col. Harry Llewellyn (*above*). A fine type of big bold Show Jumper. Represented G.B. frequently abroad and was in the winning Gold Medal team at the 1952 Olympic Games, ridden by Col. Stewart—was a member of the British Jumping team, ridden by her owner at Rome, Madrid, London and Dublin in 1951, and at Lucerne in 1952 ridden by Col. Stewart. Aherlow staged a great come-back when, ridden by Lt. Col. Harry Llewellyn, she won the Lonsdale Championship, Puissance, at the International Horse Show, White City in 1956.

BANDIT IV. Chestnut Gelding owned and ridden by Miss Ann Townsend. Bandit was bought from Sen. don Carlos Figueroa of Spain at the Horse of the Year Show, 1958, and has been jumped most successfully by Ann Townsend. In 1959 represented G.B. at Lisbon, Paris, London, Le Zoute and Rotterdam, winning many important competitions. In 1960 jumped for G.B. at Lucerne and London and was in training for a long time for the Olympic Games. At the International Horse Show at the White City in 1959 Bandit won the Lonsdale Championship, Puissance. At Rotterdam in 1959 Bandit won the Puissance and the European Ladies' Championship. Bandit will be competing for some years to come, we hope. (*illustrated*)

BANHA. Bay Gelding owned by T. Parker and ridden by Derek Kent. Banha has been amongst the big winners for the last six or seven seasons. Whilst he does not win more than his share of big competitions, if he is there he must be reckoned with. Winner of the Horse and Hound Cup at the Horse of the Year Show in 1954.

CLARE CASTLE. Brown Gelding owned and ridden by Miss Susan Cohen. This has been one of the most successful combinations of 1960. Winner of the European Ladies' Championship at Copenhagen and of the Queen Elizabeth Cup at the White City. Represented G.B. in Rome in 1961.

CRAVEN A. Bay Mare. Owned and ridden by Peter Robeson. One of the most famous and greatest hearted of all time. Reserve horse for G.B. in 1952 Olympic Games. Winner of innumerable big competitions and many times a member of Great Britain's team, including Lucerne and Dublin 1950, Nice, Rome, Dublin and Le Zoute 1951, Lucerne and London 1952, London and Dublin 1953, Lisbon, Madrid, London, Dublin 1954. Paris 1955— Winner of B.S.J.A. Eastern Counties 1955. At the Horse of the Year Show Winner of the Fred Foster Puissance 1952 and 1956, and of the Victor Ludorum 1952, and at the I.H.S. White City of the Lonsdale Championship, Puissance and the Daily Mail Cup in 1954. Retired from Show Jumping and is at Stud.

DUMBELL. Bay Gelding. Owned by L. Cawthraw and ridden by Ted Williams. Australian bred and competed in the 1956 Olympic Games for Australia in the Individual Show Jumping, ridden by Bert Jacobs. Sold by auction after the Games and bought by Mr. Cawthraw. Represented G.B. at Rome and London in 1957 and at Aachen in 1958. Winner of the Gillian McLean Puissance at Southport Flower Show in 1956, the Eastern Counties in 1957 and 1958, and the Northern in 1957 and 1959. On the latter occasion in his present ownership of Mr. D. Massarella and ridden by Michael Freer. Winner of the Leading Jumper of the Year class at the Horse of the Year Show in 1956. Still competing very successfully in his present ownership and in the hands of Michael Freer.

EARLSRATH RAMBLER. Brown Gelding owned by Capt. J. Palethorpe and ridden by Miss Jill Palethorpe (now Mrs. S. Banks) and by Miss Dawn Palethorpe, pictured (now Mrs. Warren Wofford). Another great favourite with the crowd owing to a playful kick when entering the ring. Winner of the B.S.J.A. Ladies' Championship in 1954 ridden by Dawn. Has frequently represented G.B. abroad and was the reserve horse for the 1956 Olympic Games. Winner of the Queen's Cup at the White City in 1955 and 1956. Winner of the Grand Prix in Rotterdam in 1956 and 2nd in 1957, also winning the Ladies' Championship. A member of the winning British Team in the Aga Khan Trophy in Dublin in 1956, 1958 and 1959. At the Horse of the Year Show he won the Leading Jumper of the Year in 1954 and the Victor Ludorum in 1955, ridden by Dawn. Still competing ridden by Mrs. S. Banks.

FARMER'S BOY. Bay Gelding. Owned and ridden by Harvey Smith. Has been most successful during the last few years. Winner of the National Championship in 1960 and Leading Jumper of the Year at the Horse of the Year Show 1959, Represented Great Britain in Dublin when they won the Aga Khan Trophy in 1958. Is always amongst the big winners each year and is still competing.

FINALITY, Bay Mare owned and ridden by Miss Pat Smythe. One of the first of the great jumpers to come to the front after the war. Finality was first schooled for polo and then took up Show jumping. At the Bath & West Show at Cheltenham in 1946, two horses were reported to be of great promise and these were Foxhunter and Finality. Both went with the British team to Ostend and Le Zoute in 1947, and in 1950 these two fought a tremendous duel in the Fred Foster Puissance at Harringay, eventually dividing 1st and 2nd. Later Finality was bought by Mr. Snodgrass of Scotland and in his ownership and ridden by Pat Smythe, she won the Leading Jumper of the Year award at the first Horse of the Year Show.

FLANAGAN. Chestnut Gelding. Owned by Robert Hanson and ridden by Miss Pat Smythe. Flanagan has been one of the mainstays of the British Team since 1955 and has been in the team at the last two Olympic Games. Has jumped and won in almost every country in Europe and also in U.S.A. and Canada. Owing to being abroad so much, Flanagan has not competed in very many B.S.J.A. Championships but he has won the Ladies' Championship in 1955 and 1958, the North of England in 1956, the South of England in 1957 and the Olympic Trial in 1959. At the Horse of the Year Show he won the William Hanson Trophy in 1959 and at the International Horse Show at the White City the Imperial Cup in 1955, and the Country Life and Riding Cup in 1960. He was also 2nd in the European Ladies' Championship in 1959.

FOXHUNTER. Bay Gelding, by Erehwemos, dam by Stepforward. Owned and ridden by Lt. Col. Harry Llewellyn. Probably the best known Show Jumper since 1945. The first and only horse to win the King George V Gold Cup three times. Represented Gt. Britain in the Olympic Games in 1948 and 1952 jumping a Clear Round in 1952 and assisting G.B. to win the Gold Medal. Winner of the Grand Prix Competition at almost every European International Horse Show and was the mainstay of the British team from 1948 to 1955. Competed successfully in U.S.A. and Canada. Contributed very largely towards Lt. Col. Harry Llewellyn being the Leading Show Jumping Rider in Europe 3 years in succession. B.S.J.A. National Champion in 1953. At the International Horse Show, White City, Foxhunter won the Lonsdale Championship, Puissance in 1950 and 1953 and The Daily Mail Cup in 1951. Gave his name to "The Foxhunter Competition".

FRANCO. Brown Gelding owned and ridden by David Barker. A member of the British Olympic Team in 1960 and also represented G.B. at Le Zoute and Rotterdam in 1959, Lucerne, London, and Dublin in 1960. Franco is still a young horse and with more experience will become a real front ranker. In 1958, his first serious Season, he won the Gillian McLean Puissance Competition at Southport Flower Show, and in 1959 the Lancashire Area International Trial. More successes are likely to follow.

GALWAY BOY. Brown Gelding. Owned by A. H. Payne and ridden by A. Oliver, another of Mr. Payne's great Show Jumpers. Represented G.B. at Dublin in 1950 when he was only 5 years old. Winner of the Walwyn Cup in 1954 and of the Peal Cup at Badminton 1955. Won the Daily Telegraph Cup at the Horse of the Year Show in 1951 when owned by T. Makin and ridden by S. Hayes. In 1953, Galway Boy divided first in the Lonsdale Cup Puissance at the White City with Uruguay of Italy and Foxhunter of G.B. and won the Daily Mail Cup in 1956. Galway Boy is now almost retired from Show Jumping.

GAY ROMANCE. Chestnut Gelding. Owned by T. Parker and ridden by Derek Kent. Gay Romance was one of the very many promising Novice horses produced by Len Carter. Competed very successfully ridden by Mrs. Carter before being sold to Mr. Tom Parker. Winner of many big Competitions and finished the 1960 Season amongst the first ten horses. Winner of the West of England Championship in 1958. Still competing very successfully.

HOLLANDIA. Chestnut Gelding. Owned and ridden by Mrs. Warren Wofford (née Miss Dawn Palethorpe). Hollandia is one of the most experienced horses competing today. He was originally in the U.S.A. Olympic Team until Mr. Wofford came to live in this country. In 1958 Hollandia won the William Hanson Stakes at the Horse of the Year Show ridden by Mr. Wofford who then passed the horse over to his wife. In 1959 Hollandia and Mrs. Wofford represented G.B. at Lisbon, Madrid, Paris, London and Dublin and won many competitions at these Shows. Was Reserve horse and rider for the 1960 Olympics. At the International Horse Show, White City, Hollandia won the Lonsdale Championship, Puissance, in 1959. (*illustrated*).

HOLYWELL SURPRISE. Grey Gelding owned and ridden by Miss Dawn Palethorpe (now Mrs. Warren Wofford). Represented Great Britain abroad in 1956 and 1957. Winner of the White City Stadium Cup at the International Horse Show at the White City 1955 and 1957 and at the Horse of the Year Show won the Daily Telegraph Cup in 1955, the Beaufort Stakes and the County Life & Riding Cup in 1956. *(illustrated left)*

JANE SUMMERS. Chestnut Mare. Owned and ridden by Ted Edgar. A most gallant little mare which has won against the best. A big winner at home and has competed successfully abroad with the British Team. B.S.J.A. National Championship winner in 1957, the Horse and Hound Cup in 1956, The West of England in 1958, The South of England in 1959 and the Welsh in 1960. Leading Jumper of the Year at the Horse of the Year Show 1958. Still competing.

JOHN GILPIN. Brown Gelding owned by A. H. Payne and ridden by Alan Oliver. Another most successful member of Mr. Payne's string of Jumpers. Winner of B.S.J.A. National Championship in 1959, Eastern Counties 1954 and The Peal Cup in 1957. Is always amongst the big winners each year and is still competing. *(illustrated right)*

MONTY. Bay/Brown Gelding. Owned by Mr. E. M. Broad and ridden mainly by Lt. Col. Harry Llewellyn. Probably the greatest "Speed" horse in Europe during 1949-52, winning a large number of competitions all over Europe and contributing largely towards Lt. Col. Harry Llewellyn being the Leading Show Jumping Rider in Europe 3 years in succession. Represented G.B. in the Olympic Games in 1948 when ridden by Major Arthur Carr. Bought in Ireland during the war and was a big winner in the North before becoming a member of the British Team. Is now retired at Mr. Broad's farm in Cheshire.
(*illustrated*)

MR. POLLARD. Chestnut Gelding. Owned by J. King and ridden by Miss Pat Smythe and later by Ted Williams. Produced as a Novice by John Walmsley as Gilpin II and represented G.B. at Geneva in 1957 ridden by him. In Mr. King's ownership and ridden by Miss Smythe, Mr. Pollard won the B.S.J.A. Ladies' Championship in 1959 and the North of England Championship in 1958. At the Horse of the Year Show Mr. Pollard won the Leading Show Jumper of the Year in 1958 and in the same year the Queen's Cup at the International Horse Show at the White City. Still competing successfully.

NIZEFELA. Bay or Brown Gelding. Owned and ridden by W. H. White. Nizefela has been one of the greatest Show Jumpers of all time. Starting soon after the war, he quickly came to the fore and in his career has won many big competitions, but it is as a "team" horse that he has made his name. He and his rider have many times been referred to as "the full back" of the British Team. Nizefela assisted in the winning of the Gold Medal at the Olympic Games in 1952 and the Bronze Medal at Stockholm in 1956. He has represented Great Britain in no less than 23 Nations Cup Competitions, including 3 in U.S.A. and Canada. Winner of the Walwyn Cup in 1950 and 1953, the North of England in 1953 and 1955, The Midland in 1954 and 1957, and The Welsh in 1957. At the Horse of the Year Show in 1954 he won the Fred Foster Puissance. Nizefela is still competing.

NOBBLER. Bay Gelding, owned and ridden by Miss Mary Whitehead (now Mrs. Brian Marshall). Nobbler represented Great Britain on many occasions when ridden by his owner and also when generously loaned by her to other riders. Reserve horse for the 1952 Olympic Games. Competed in the British Team at home and abroad from 1951 until 1957.

NUGGET. Dark Chestnut Gelding. Owned by Miss Ann Morley–*illustrated*–(now Mrs. John Walmsley) and ridden by John Walmsley. Nugget has been one of the great "characters" in Show Jumping, and few horses have been more popular with the crowd. In conformation he is a big heavyweight cob with a docked tail. He has often been referred to as "The Rocking Horse" from the way he jumps straight up and down, but he has astounded his critics by being able to clear the largest of spread fences. Nugget won the B.S.J.A. Ladies' Championship in 1956, the Walwyn Cup in 1957 and at the Horse of the Year Show he won the Horse and Hound Cup in 1955 and 1956 and the Victor Ludorum in 1958. Probably his greatest performance was at the Harewood Horse Trials in 1956 when he won on all three days including the Ladies' Championship ridden by his Owner and the Cock o' the North Championship, when ridden by John Walmsley. Nugget is now semi-retired on the Walmsleys' farm in Yorkshire.

D.R.—D

OORSKEIT. Chestnut Gelding. Owned and ridden by Lady Sarah Fitzalan-Howard. Brought over from South Africa in 1958 and jumped with success by Miss Gonda Butters, winning the Lonsdale Memorial Stakes at the Horse of the Year Show. Since then has been right to the fore with the present owner and is likely to continue so. Competed abroad at Le Zoute and Rotterdam in 1959 winning two competitions and at Lucerne in 1960.

PEGASUS XIII. Grey Gelding. Owned by L. Cawthraw and ridden by Ted Williams. The outstanding combination of the last few years during which time they have won almost all the big competitions and have been amongst the biggest winners. Winner of B.S.J.A. National Championship 1956, North of England 1956, Midland 1960, Horse & Hound 1957, 1958, 1960. Leading Jumper of the Year at Horse of the Year Show, 1957 and 1960. Competed in U.S.A. and Canada in 1957 and won the Grand Prix at all three International Shows, Harrisburg, New York and Toronto. Still competing with great success.
(illustrated)

PRINCE HAL. Chestnut Gelding, by Hallowmas. Owned and ridden by Miss Pat Smythe. Bought off the Race Course when it was considered he would not win Steeplechases. Represented G.B. on many occasions and was one of the most brilliant and spectacular Jumpers of the century. Prince Hal won big competitions in almost every country in Europe and competed successfully in U.S.A. and Canada. Won the B.S.J.A. Ladies' Championship in 1952 and again in 1957, the West of England in 1951, The Midland in 1952, The Welsh and the South of England in 1956. Also the Victor Ludorum at the Horse of the Year Show in 1955 and the Daily Mail Cup at I.H.S. White City in 1955 and 1957.

RED ADMIRAL. Chestnut Gelding. Owned by A. H. Payne and ridden by Alan Oliver. In his day Red Admiral was one of the greatest British Jumpers and took part in many a tussle against the best International horses at the International Shows at White City, Harringay and Wembley. Winner of the B.S.J.A. National Championship in 1951 and 1954. The Northern in 1960, the Walwyn Championship 1954, and the Harry Hall Trophy 1952. Leading Jumper of the Year at Horse of the Year Show 1953 and winner of the Fred Foster Puissance in 1955, 1957 and 1958. Red Admiral is still competing, though not as regularly as earlier in his career. (*illustrated*)

RED STAR II. Bay Gelding. Owned by A. H. Payne and ridden by A. Oliver. The first of Mr. Payne's really great Show Jumpers and from 1946 to 1955 was always amongst the Season's biggest winners. Winner of Welsh Championship in 1949, the Harry Hall Trophy 1952, the Peal Cup at Badminton 1953 and the South of England Championship in 1954 and 1955. Represented G.B. in London and at Geneva in 1951. Now almost retired at Mr. Oliver's farm in Bucks., but has come out towards the end of each Season including 1960 and has always won at least one competition.

ROYAL LORD, Bay Gelding. Owned by J. C. Howard and ridden by G. Hobbs. Royal Lord won the Daily Express Foxhunter Championship in 1955 ridden by his first owner, Miss B. Rose. Has since progressed right to the top and is now a first ranker. Winner of the B.S.J.A. Midlands Championship in 1958 and many other good Competitions. Represented G.B. at Dublin in 1958, and Geneva in 1959. At the Horse of the Year Show won the Lonsdale Memorial Stakes in 1957 and the Daily Telegraph Cup in 1959 and the White City Stadium Cup at the International Horse Show in 1958. Competed in Rome in 1961.

SCORCHIN. Bay Mare owned by The Hon. D. Paget and ridden by Peter Robeson, W. H. White (pictured) and Miss Pat Smythe. Brought out by Ted Williams who sold Scorchin to Miss Paget. Loaned by her to the British Team and competed in the 1956 Olympic Games ridden by Peter Robeson winning a Bronze Medal. Represented G.B. at Ostend in 1954 and Dublin in 1955 ridden by Susan Whitehead, the team being second on both occasions. Ridden by Peter Robeson at Lucerne and Stockholm in 1956. In 1960 was Miss Smythe's reserve horse at the Olympic Games and won the Daily Mail Cup at the White City for her that year. On Miss Paget's death, Scorchin was bought by Miss Smythe in whose ownership she will continue to jump.

SMOKY BOB. Grey Gelding. Owned and ridden by Marshal Charlesworth. Represented G.B. in Dublin 1958, Le Zoute and Rotterdam 1959. Winner of many good competitions, and still competing.

SNOWSTORM. Grey Gelding. Owned by Robert Hanson and ridden by the late Bill Hanson. Brought out by Andrew Massarella and Sons. Won Leading Jumper of the Year Class at the Horse of the Year Show in 1952 the first time Bill Hanson competed in it. Was retired from Show Jumping shortly after.

STONE PARK. Bay mare owned by F. D. Wright and ridden by Basil Hales. Stone Park is said to have graded into "A" in one day in Ireland before being brought to England by Mrs. A. G. Dickinson and later bought by Mr. Wright for whom she won the Eastern Counties Championship in 1959 and both the Gillian McLean Puissance at Southport Flower Show and the South of England at Brighton in 1960. Still competing with success.
(*illustrated*)

SUDDEN. Bay Gelding. Owned and ridden by Miss Mary Barnes. Sudden has been a front rank jumper since 1955 at which time he was ridden by Tom Barnes and represented G.B. at Le Zoute and Rotterdam. In 1956 represented G.B. at Ostend and Rotterdam, and in 1957 at Rome. He was then taken over by Mary Barnes and competed at Ostend and Rotterdam in 1958. Winner of the Country Life and Riding Cup at the International Horse Show, White City in 1959. Sudden is probably the most versatile horse jumping today. He can compete with an equal chance of success in a Puissance or a Speed Competition and has won both. Still competing very successfully and represented G.B. in Rome in May 1961.

SUNSALVE. Chestnut Gelding. Owned by Mr. Oliver Anderson and ridden first by Miss Elizabeth Anderson (pictured) and later by David Broome. Sunsalve, in the last year, has probably made the greatest impact on Show Jumping of any horse since Foxhunter. It is interesting that both were bred in Norfolk and ridden by residents of Monmouthshire. Sunsalve will be best known for his Bronze Medal in the Individual Show Jumping Competition at the 1960 Olympics and for his brilliant second round in the Grand Prix des Nations which was at first recorded as the only clear round in the competition, but later amended to 4 faults for a foot in the water jump. Another unique performance is that he won the Queen's Cup at the International Horse Show in 1957 when ridden by Elizabeth Anderson and the King George V Cup in 1960, ridden by David Broome. Elizabeth also won the Fred Foster Puissance on him at the Horse of the Year Show in 1956. In 1960 he won the Fred Foster Puissance and the Victor Ludorum at the Horse of the Year Show with David Broome. Sunsalve is still comparatively young and has many more fields of conquest open to him.

THE MONARCH. Black Gelding. Owned and ridden by the late Bill Hanson and afterwards ridden by Peter Robeson. Represented G.B. at Rotterdam and Geneva ridden by Andrew Massarella Jun. in 1951. In 1952 competed for G.B. in Rotterdam and in 1953 at Nice and Rome ridden by his owner. Won the Rome Grand Prix in 1953, the only time it has ever been won by a British competitor. In the same year was in the winning team at Dublin and competed in U.S.A. and Canada. At the Horse of the Year Show won the London Stakes ridden by Peter Robeson in 1955. Has now been retired by Mrs. William Hanson to her home in Ireland. Ridden in the illustration by Col. Llewellyn.

TIM II. Bay Gelding. Owned by T. Mulholland and ridden by Paddy MacMahon. Has been jumping and winning against the best since 1946. B.S.J.A. National Champion 1958, winner of The Midland Championship 1947, 1948, 1956, 1959 and 1960, and The Eastern Counties 1950. Tim II has competed at every Horse of the Year Show since its inception in 1949. Was lent to Ted Williams to take to U.S.A. and Canada 1957 where he jumped very successfully. Still competing.

TOSCA. Grey Mare. Owned and ridden by Miss Pat Smythe. During 1952 and 1953 Tosca was the most consistent jumper in England and won almost every big National Competition during her career. Frequently represented G.B. at home and abroad. Won the B.S.J.A. Ladies' Championship in 1953, the North of England in 1952 and 1954, The Midland and also South of England 1952 and the West of England Championship in 1953. Was winner of the Victor Ludorum at the Horse of the Year Show 1954. Retired to stud and has bred 3 foals to date.

TRUEMAN II. Bay Gelding. Owned and ridden by Bay Lane. Another very versatile Jumper, having won a Puissance and a Speed Competition on the same day. One of the best speed horses now competing. Winner of the London Stakes in 1959 at the Horse of the Year Show.

VENUS III. Bay Mare. Owned and ridden by Mrs. George Boon. Bred by Owner, a good winner for the last 3 or 4 years. At the International Horse Show at the White City winner of the Country Life and Riding Cup in 1958. Still competing.

YORKSHIREMAN. Brown Gelding. Owned by L. Cawthraw and ridden by Ted Williams. A comparative newcomer to big jumping. Has made a most promising start and won the Eastern Counties Championship in 1959 and both the West of England and the Midland in 1960. At the Horse of the Year Show in 1960 won the Sunday Times Cup.

Has now been bought by Miss Anne Townsend, and a most successful career is promised.

Wildfire III ridden by David Broome.

WILDFIRE III. Bay Gelding. Owned by F. M. Broome and ridden by David Broome. This has proved to be a wonderfully successful combination and has been right to the fore the last three years. Wildfire was David Broome's reserve horse for the 1960 Olympic Games. Represented G.B. at Rotterdam in 1959 and at Lucerne in 1960. Winner of both Welsh Championships in 1958. At the Horse of the Year Show in 1959 Wildfire won the Lonsdale Memorial Stakes and the Horse and Hound Cup. Wildfire and David Broome are still competing with success. (*illustrated left*)

WORKBOY. Black Gelding. Owned and ridden by Brig. C. H. Blacker. Workboy used to be one of the best 2 Mile chasers and was only trained for Show Jumping quite late in life. He has reached the top in both spheres. Owing to Brigadier Blacker's military commitments, Workboy's appearances have been limited, but he represented G.B. in Lisbon and Madrid in 1959 and was in training for the Olympic Games in 1960. At the International Horse Show at the White City in 1959 Workboy won the Imperial Cup. They represented G.B. in Rome in 1961.

CHAPTER TEN

The Principal Horse, Agricultural and Horticultural Shows

NOTE: The list has been compiled chronologically by the months in which the Shows are normally held.

APRIL

MELTON CONSTABLE JUMPING SHOW: The Hon. Mrs. A. Baillie, Melton Constable Park, Norfolk.

HICKSTEAD SHOW: at All England Jumping Course, Hickstead. Miss P. Parsons, Hickstead Place, Hickstead, Sussex.

BADMINTON HORSE TRIALS: Enquiries to The B.S.J.A., 16 Bedford Square, London, W.C.1.

ASCOT JUMPING SHOW: Lady S. Fitzalan Howard, Arundel, Sussex.

AYRSHIRE COUNTY SHOW: S. Gilmour, 32 Beresford Terrace, Ayr, Scotland.

MAY

ALDERSHOT SHOW: Lt. Col. R. K. Chiesman, Show Offices, Steele's Road, Aldershot, Hants.

NEWARK AND NOTTS COUNTY SHOW: J. Crocker, Besthorpe, Newark, Notts.

OXFORDSHIRE COUNTY SHOW: Mrs. J. E. Bridgewater, 269 Banbury Road, Oxford.

DUNBARTONSHIRE AGRICULTURAL SOCIETY: A. R. Scott, National Commercial Bank of Scotland Ltd., Alexandria, Dunbartonshire.

LIBERATION DAY HORSE SHOW: at St. Andrew's Park, St. Helier. Mrs. J. S. O. Arthur, Les Ruettes, St. John, Jersey, C.I.

ROYAL WINDSOR HORSE SHOW: at Home Park. F. Burgess, Royal Windsor Horse Show Club, 4 Sheet Street, Windsor.

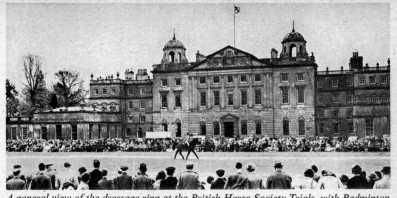

A general view of the dressage ring at the British Horse Society Trials, with Badminton House in the background.

SHROPSHIRE & WEST MIDLANDS AGRICULTURAL SOCIETY SHOW: at Permanent Showground, Shrewsbury. Lt. Col. G. R. Ellis, E.R.D., 9/11 Talbot Chambers, Shrewsbury, Shropshire.

HERTFORDSHIRE COUNTY SHOW: at Beech Farm, St. Albans. H. F. Barker, 26a Chequer Street, St. Albans, Hertfordshire.

DEVON COUNTY SHOW: at Exeter. C. F. J. Hocken, 5 Northernhay Place, Exeter, Devon.

WARWICKSHIRE COUNTY SHOW: at Wellesbourne Aerodrome, nr. Warwick. John Staite, 7 Euston Place, Leamington Spa, Warwickshire.

ARMY 3-DAY EVENT: at Tidworth. Major T. J. C. Washington, IX/XII

Royal Lancers, H.Q. R.A.C. 3 Div., Tidworth, Hants.

DERBYSHIRE COUNTY SHOW: at Bretby Park, nr. Burton-on-Trent. S. T. Parker, Agricultural Office, Cattle Market, Derby.

SURREY COUNTY SHOW: at Stoke Park, Guildford. J. A. Chiles, 12 Bell Street, Reigate, Surrey.

STAFFORDSHIRE COUNTY SHOW: at Stafford. W. V. Prestwood, Knowle Wall, Trentham, Stoke-on-Trent.

RICHMOND ROYAL HORSE SHOW: L. F. Lorkin, 42 Shaftesbury Road, Richmond, Surrey.

HICKSTEAD SHOW: at All England Jumping Course, Hickstead. Miss P. Parsons, Hickstead Place, Hickstead, Sussex.

SUFFOLK COUNTY SHOW: at Ipswich. H. A. Byford, 30 Museum Street, Ipswich, Suffolk.

BATH AND WEST SHOW: at Bristol. J. G. Yardley, O.B.E. 3 Pierrepoint Street, Bath, Somerset.

JUNE

ROYAL CORNWALL AGRICULTURAL ASSOCIATION SHOW: at Wadebridge.

A. H. Riddle, R.C.A.A., 4 Upper Lemon Villas, Truro, Cornwall.

CHESHIRE COUNTY SHOW: at Hooton Park, nr. Chester. F. Hughes, 4a Hunter Street, Chester.

ESSEX COUNTY SHOW: at Great Leighs, nr. Chelmsford. J. A. Pollard, 13 King Edward Avenue, Chelmsford, Essex.

LEICESTERSHIRE COUNTY SHOW: at Braunstone Aerodrome. T. W. Garton, 39 London Road, Leicester.

HICKSTEAD SHOW: at All England Jumping Course, Hickstead, Sussex. Miss P. Parsons, Hickstead Place, Hickstead, Sussex.

The Royal Windsor Horse Show held in May of each year.

THREE COUNTIES AGRICULTURAL SHOW: at Malvern, Worcs. G. Hastings, Three Counties Show, Malvern, Worcs.

SUSSEX COUNTY SHOW: at Haywards Heath. C. Young, Southdown House, Chichester, Sussex.

NORTHERN INTERNATIONAL HORSE SHOW: at White City, Manchester. The Secretary General, B.S.J.A., 16 Bedford Square, London, W.C.1.

HUNTINGDONSHIRE COUNTY SHOW: at Hinchingbrook Park. E. A. Carr, Porch House, Great Gransden, Sandy, Beds.

HICKSTEAD SHOW: at All England Jumping Course, Hickstead, Sussex. Miss P. Parsons, Hickstead Place, Hickstead, Sussex.

ROYAL HIGHLAND SHOW: at Ingliston, nr. Edinburgh. R. M. Lemmon, O.B.E., B.L., 8 Eglinton Crescent, Edinburgh, 12, Scotland.

ROYAL COUNTIES AGRICULTURAL SOCIETY: Col. S. C. Rigby Dale, O.B.E., 12 Wote Street, Basingstoke, Hants.

LINCOLNSHIRE AGRICULTURAL SHOW: B. Shelley, Westminster Bank Chambers, 8 Guildhall Street, Lincoln.

ROYAL NORFOLK AGRICULTURAL SHOW: at Norwich. H. E. Jeffrey, Diss, Norfolk.

UNITED EAST LOTHIAN AGRICULTURAL SOCIETY SHOW: at Somnerfield Park, Haddington. Stirling & Burnet, Solicitors, Haddington, East Lothian.

HICKSTEAD SHOW: at All England Jumping Course, Hickstead, Sussex. Miss P. Parsons, Hickstead Place, Hickstead, Sussex.

THE ROYAL SHOW: at Cambridge. Alec Hobson, M.V.O., O.B.E., Royal Agricultural Society of England, 35 Belgrave Square, London, S.W.1.

HICKSTEAD SHOW: at All England Jumping Course, Hickstead, Sussex. Miss P. Parsons, Hickstead, Sussex.

GREAT YORKSHIRE SHOW: at Harrogate. F. M. Baldwin, M.B.E., B.Sc., Cliftonfield, Shipton Road, York.

KENT COUNTY AGRICULTURAL SHOW: at Mote Park, Maidstone. W. M. Wallis, "Merristone", Pluckley, nr. Ashford, Kent.

THE LIVERPOOL SHOW: at Wavertree, Liverpool. Thomas Alker, Show Offices, 40 Victoria Street, Liverpool.

BEDFORDSHIRE AGRICULTURAL SHOW: at Cardington Road, Bedford. Leslie J.

Gay Time III lands safely over the jump at the Royal International Horse Show at the White City.

Swaffield, Market Place, Ampthill, Bedford.

NORTHUMBERLAND COUNTY SHOW: at Hulne Park, Alnwick, John Ellerington, Rothley Lodge, Hartburn, Morpeth, Northumberland.

HICKSTEAD SHOW: at Hickstead Place, Sussex. Miss P. Parsons, Hickstead Place, Hickstead, Sussex.

TUNBRIDGE WELLS & SOUTH EASTERN COUNTIES AGRICULTURAL SHOW: at Show Ground, Eridge Road, Tunbridge Wells. Mrs. E. F. Hart, 12 Lonsdale Gardens, Tunbridge Wells.

PETERBOROUGH SHOW: at Show Ground, Eastfield, Peterborough. R. W. Bird, Agricultural Office, 12 Priestgate, Peterborough, Northants.

THE NORTHERN COUNTIES AGRICULTURAL SHOW: at Bught Park, Inverness. D. M. Duncan, National Commercial Bank Buildings, Fraser Street, Inverness.

CUMBERLAND AGRICULTURAL SHOW: at Bitts Park, Carlisle. J. M. A. Errington, 57 English Street, Carlisle.

CITY OF MANCHESTER HORSE SHOW: at Platt Fields Park, Manchester, 15. Peter Grainger, c/o 165 Stretford Road, Manchester, 15.

ROYAL INTERNATIONAL HORSE SHOW: at White City Stadium. J. E. Blackmore, 16 Bedford Square, London, W.C.1.

ROYAL WELSH AGRICULTURAL SHOW: at Golden Grove, Llandilo, Carmarthen. J. A. George, Royal Welsh Agricultural Society, Queen's Road, Aberystwyth.

MORAYSHIRE AGRICULTURAL SOCIETY: A. L. Falconer, 54 High Street, Elgin, Morayshire, Scotland.

BORDER UNION SHOW: at Springwood Park, Kelso. John T. Laing, 30 Square, Kelso, Roxburghshire.

DUMFRIES AGRICULTURAL SHOW: at the Showfield Park Farm. H. B. Hewat, 8 English Street, Dumfries, Scotland.

NORTH LONSDALE AGRICULTURAL SHOW: at Uplands, Crossamorr, Ulverston, Lancs. G. Fox, 14 Swarthdale Avenue, Ulverston, Lancs.

A Member of the Spanish Riding School in Vienna.

AUGUST

ROYAL LANCASHIRE AGRICULTURAL SHOW: at Blackpool. The Secretary, Derby House, 12 Winckley Square, Preston, Lancs.

ABERGAVENNY AND BORDER COUNTIES SHOW: at Glebe Lands, Llanwenarth Citra, nr. Abergavenny. D. E. Thomas, F.A.L.P.A., Newmarket Chambers, Abergavenny, Monmouthshire.

NORTH WALES AGRICULTURAL SOCIETY SHOW: at Rhosdican Fields, Caernarvon. E. W. Williams, 2 Hill Street, Caernarvon.

SHEFFIELD SHOW: at Endcliffe Park, Sheffield, 11. F. A. Pollard, Manager,

Parks, Cemeteries and Allotments Dept., 125 Norfolk Street, Sheffield, 1.

DURHAM COUNTY SHOW: at Lambton Park, Chester-le-Street. L. Rudd, 27 Sutton Street, Durham.

KINGSTON UPON HULL SHOW: H. Dawson, Dacre Farm, Brandesburton, Driffield, Yorks.

COUNTY OF LONDON HORSE SHOW: at Clapham Common. The B.S.J.A., 16 Bedford Square, London, W.C.1.

RUTLAND COUNTY SHOW: at Oakham. John Fletcher, B.A., Station Road, Oakham, Rutland.

BILSTON HORTICULTURAL SHOW: at Hickman Park, Bilston. H. Arnall, 52 Prouds Lane, Bilston, Staffs.

EVESHAM HORSE AND CATTLE SHOW: at Crown Meadow, Evesham. John E. Liley, Westington Mill, Chipping Campden, Glos.

CITY OF LEICESTER SHOW: at Abbey Park, Leicester. Mrs. D. M. Toms, 82 Rosemead Drive, Oadby, Leics.

BAKEWELL SHOW: at the Permanent Show Ground, Bakewell. W. A. Conway, The Farmers' Club Offices, Devonshire Chambers, Bakewell, Derbyshire.

DENBIGHSHIRE AND FLINTSHIRE CENTENARY SHOW: at Prestatyn, Flintshire. W. E. Glover, Esq., Midland Bank Chambers, High Street, Holywell.

HICKSTEAD SHOW: at All England Jumping Course, Hickstead, Sussex. Miss P. Parsons, Hickstead Place, Hickstead, Sussex.

CANNOCK CHASE COLLIERY SPORTS SHOW: at Cannock Chase Collieries Sports Ground. J. W. Earp, 177 High Street, Chasetown, Walsall, Staffs.

KINROSS-SHIRE AGRICULTURAL SHOW: at Kinross House, Kinross. J. F. Watson, M.R.C.V.S., Ardmhor, Stirling Road, Milnathort, Kinross-shire.

ANGLESEY AGRICULTURAL SHOW: at Bodwina, Gwalchmai. R. Ll. Edwards, Hensio, Llanghffo, Gaerwen, Anglesey.

SHREWSBURY MUSICAL AND FLORAL FETE: at The Quarry, Shrewsbury, Shropshire. J. C. Tipton, 9 The Square, Shrewsbury, Shropshire.

BRIGHTON HORSE SHOW & SOUTH OF ENGLAND JUMPING CHAMPIONSHIPS: at Brighton Sports Arena, Tongdean Lane, Brighton. G. Hume, Director of Entertainments & Publicity, Royal York Bdgs., Brighton, Sussex.

A general view of the closing ceremony at the Horse of the Year Show.

CONSETT & DISTRICT EXHIBITION AND SHOW: at Belle Vue Park, Consett. G. W. Robson, Council offices, Medomsley Road, Consett, Co. Durham.

SOUTHPORT FLOWER SHOW: at Victoria Park, Southport. G. W. Nicholls, Flower Show Department, Victoria Bdgs., Lord Street, Southport, Lancs.

BRITISH TIMKEN SHOW: at Duston, Northampton. Lt. Col. A. T. Roper-Caldbeck, British Timken, Duston, Northampton.

MONMOUTHSHIRE SHOW: at Racecourse, Vauxhall, Monmouthshire. Ben Breakwell, Hadnock Court, Monmouth.

SEPTEMBER

CITY OF BIRMINGHAM SHOW: at Handsworth Park, Birmingham. G. E. Ross, General Manager, Parks Department, Civic Centre, Birmingham, 1.

HICKSTEAD SHOW: at All England Jumping Course, Hickstead, Sussex. Miss P. Parsons, Hickstead Place, Hickstead, Sussex.

BUCKS COUNTY SHOW: at Hartwell Park, Aylesbury. John Barr, F.A.I., 2 Church Street, Aylesbury, Bucks.

HICKSTEAD SHOW: at All England Jumping Course, Hickstead, Sussex. Miss P. Parsons, Hickstead Place, Hickstead, Sussex.

MERIONETH AGRICULTURAL SOCIETY COUNTY SHOW: H. R. Davies, Fron Hyfryd, Bala, Merioneth.

NORTHAMPTONSHIRE AGRICULTURAL SHOW: at Overstone Park, nr. Northampton. L. E. Deacon, Redlands, Cliftonville, Northampton.

MONTGOMERYSHIRE SHOW: at Welshpool. Morris, Marshall & Poole, Welshpool.

WESTMORLAND COUNTY AGRICULTURAL SHOW: at Kendal, Westmorland. Alan S. Thomas, F.A.I., 37 Stramongate, Kendal, Westmorland.

THAME SHOW: at Risborough Road, Thame. K. W. Arnold, 11 Buttermarket, Thame, Oxon.

WOKINGHAM & DISTRICT AGRICULTURAL SHOW: at Worton Grange, Basingstoke Road, Reading. J. E. Batting, 12 Station Road, Reading, Berks.

OCTOBER

HORSE OF THE YEAR SHOW: at The Empire Pool, Wembley. J. E. Blackmore, 16 Bedford Square, London, W.C.1.

CHAPTER ELEVEN

Combined Training

Combined training was first introduced as an Equestrian Event in the Olympic Games in 1912 as "Concours Complet". At that time it was considered to be a test of the perfect Officer's Charger, and bore the name "The Military". The Event has changed very little since its

Miss Sheila Wilcox competing at Badminton.

inception. When the Olympic Games were allocated to London in 1948 the "Concours Complet" or Three-Day Event as it became known in England, was held at Aldershot. The Duke of Beaufort was much impressed with the event and offered the British Horse Society the use of Badminton Park for the holding of a Three-Day Event each year to assist in the selection of Riders and Horses for future Olympic Games. This has been held annually since 1949. At Helsinki in 1952 Great Britain was well represented and was unlucky not to be awarded a medal but, owing to a fall "on the flat", a rider was concussed and went the wrong side of a turning flag and the team was disqualified. In 1956 in Stockholm, Great Britain won the Team Gold Medal for this event.

Combined Training is a comprehensive test of horse and rider. The horse

121

must be fit, supple and obedient, possessing stamina and speed; the rider must be able to train and condition his horse in order to produce its best performance; both must have spirit and courage and a mutual confidence and understanding.

The principal Combined Training Competition is known as The Three-Day Event, in which the same horse and rider undergo three distinct tests on three consecutive days.

DRESSAGE

A series of exercises to test the horse's training and obedience, marked by a panel of Judges.

SPEED, ENDURANCE and CROSS-COUNTRY

A 13-25 mile route, partly along roads and tracks, partly over a steeplechase course and partly across country with fixed, natural obstacles, to be completed within a stipulated time, penalties being incurred for falls and disobediences at the obstacles.

JUMPING

A Jumping test in an Arena.

Of these, the exacting test on the second day is the most important. The dressage test is to show the horse has acquired the requisite standard of training and obedience, while the jumping test is simply to prove that, despite the great demands made upon him, he is fit and supple enough to continue in service.

Olympic and International Three-Day Events are controlled by the Fédération Equestre Internationale (F.E.I.) but the British Horse Society, as National Federation affiliated to the F.E.I. is the governing body in this country.

Since the inauguration of Badminton the sport of Combined Training has grown in popularity among both competitors and spectators. The standard rose each year and in 1953 Badminton was appointed the first European Championships (held in a different country each year) under the auspices of the F.E.I. In 1953 another Three-Day Event was started at Harewood in Yorkshire by gracious permission of H.R.H. The Princess Royal. The interest taken by H.M. The Queen has been a great encouragement; in 1955

Her Majesty allowed the European Championships to be held in Windsor Great Park; in 1956 her horse, Countryman, was in the British team which won the Olympic Gold Medal at Stockholm. In order to prepare horses and riders for the two major annual events, the B.H.S. instituted similar competitions on a smaller scale, known as Horse Trials, of which about 20 are now organised up and down the country each year. These, like the Three-Day Events, comprise Dressage, Cross-country and Jumping tests, but the cross-country course is much shorter and the whole competition can be completed in one day.

There are three classes in Horse Trials; Preliminary, Intermediate and Open. Thus a Competitor may proceed by carefully-planned stages from his first simple competition as a Novice to a full scale Three-Day Event, where he may come to the notice of the selectors for International trial.

In cases where entries are unlikely to be sufficient for separate Open and Intermediate Classes, permission may be obtained from the British Horse Society for these two to be combined in an UNRESTRICTED CLASS—open to all grades of horses and held under the conditions laid down for an Intermediate Class.

JUDGING COMBINED TRAINING HORSE TRIALS

DRESSAGE

is judged under the rules contained in the B.H.S. "Notes on Dressage", except where modified below.

Test Open Class—Elementary Dressage Test, unless permission has been granted by the B.H.S. for the use of a different test of equal or greater difficulty.

Intermediate Class. Novice Dressage Test.

Preliminary Class. Preliminary Dressage Test.

Penalties

First error of course	*2 penalties*
Second ,, ,, ,,	*5 penalties*
Third ,, ,, ,,	*10 penalties*
Fourth ,, ,, ,,	*Elimination*
Every commenced second in excess of the Time Allowed	$\frac{1}{2}$ (·5) *penalty*

Lt. Col. H. M. V. Nicoll, an Olympic Jumper.

SHOW JUMPING

One round of the course judged under F.E.I. Rules, Table "A", except where modified below. There is no Jump-off.

Course. The course will be simple and straightforward and about 600 yards in length. The plan of the course, showing the Time Allowed, must be posted up not less than an hour before.

Obstacles. There will be approximately 8-10 including at least one double, as solid and imposing looking as possible.

Speed. Open Class 382 yards (350 metres) per minute. Intermediate and Preliminary 327 yards (300 metres) per minute.

Penalties

First disobedience	*5 penalties*
Knocking down an obstacle	*5 penalties*
Touching boundary mark of water or feet in the water or ditch	*5 penalties*
Second disobedience in whole test	*10 penalties*
Third disobedience in whole test	*20 penalties*
Fourth disobedience in whole test	*Elimination*
Fall of horse and/or rider	*15 penalties*
For every commenced second in excess of Time Allowed	$\frac{1}{4}$ (*·25*) penalty
Exceeding the Time Limit	*Elimination*
Knocking down a boundary flag	*1 penalty*

CROSS COUNTRY

Course. Open and Intermediate—not less than 2 miles nor more than 2½ miles long with 8-12 obstacles to the mile. Preliminary. Not less than 1 mile nor more than 1¾ miles with 16-20 obstacles.

Obstacles must be solid, fixed and imposing. No obstacles will exceed a height of 3' 11" Open, 3' 9" Intermediate, 3' 6" Preliminary. Obstacles with a spread only (stream, ditch etc.) will not exceed a spread of 12' Open and Intermediate, 9' Preliminary. Obstacles with both height and spread (oxer, open ditch etc.) will not exceed a spread of:—

6' 6" at highest point	
8' at base	Open
5' 6" at highest point	
8' at base	Intermediate
4' at highest point	
7' at base	Preliminary

Horse and rider take this cross-country obstacle with ease.

125

Mr. E. Lanz on Baron jumping out of the water jump at the Harewood Horse Trials European Championships.

Speed. Minimum Time for Course calculated at 656 yards per minute for Open and Intermediate and 575 yards per minute for Preliminary. Exceeding the Minimum Time incurs ·3 penalties per second up to the Time Limit which is twice the Minimum Time.

Penalties

First refusal, run-out, circle of horse at obstacle	*20 penalties*
Second refusal, run-out, circle of horse at same obstacle	*40 penalties*

Third refusal, run-out, circle of horse at same obstacle	*80 penalties*
Fourth refusal, run-out, circle of horse at same obstacle	*Elimination*
Fall of horse and/or rider at obstacle	*60 penalties*
Knocking down boundary flag	*4 penalties*
Omission of obstacle or boundary flag	*4 penalties*

There are Hunter Trials for the Pony Clubs too!

Error of Course not rectified	
Re-taking an obstacle already jumped	} *Elimination*
Jumping obstacle in wrong order	

These penalties are cumulative.

For every second in excess of Minimum Time	*·3 penalties*
Exceeding the Time Limit	*Elimination*

COMBINED COMPETITIONS

These consist of Dressage and Show Jumping Tests which must be taken in that order. The same horse and rider must complete both tests and elimination from one test involves elimination from the whole competition. The penalties incurred for Show Jumping are deducted from the marks awarded for the dressage test. The Competitor with the highest final score is the winner. There are two classes of Combined Competition:

Open Class.

Intermediate Class—restricted to horses which, at starting, have won a total

127

of less than £40 in prize money at Official Horse Trials and Three-Day Events.

DRESSAGE

is judged under the rules contained in the B.H.S. "Notes on Dressage", except where modified below.

Test. Open Class. B.H.S. Elementary Dressage Test.

Intermediate Class. B.H.S. Novice Dressage Test.

Penalties

First error of Course	*2 penalties*
Second ,, ,, ,,	*5 penalties*
Third ,, ,, ,,	*10 penalties*
Fourth ,, ,, ,,	*Elimination*
Every commenced second in excess of the Time Allowed	*½ penalty*

SHOW JUMPING

One round of the course judged under F.E.I. Rules, Table "A", except where modified below. There is no Jump-off.

Course. The Course should be approximately 500 yards long with the obstacles so placed that the average horse should meet them in his stride. The plan of the course, showing the Time Allowed, must be posted up not less than an hour before.

Obstacles. There will be approximately 8-12 including at least one double, as solid and imposing as possible.

Speed. Open Class—382 yards per minute. Intermediate Class—327 yards per minute.

Penalties

First disobedience	*10 penalties*
Knocking down an obstacle	*10 penalties*
Touching boundary mark of water, or feet in the water or in the ditch	*10 penalties*
Second disobedience in whole test	*20 penalties*
Third disobedience in whole test	*40 penalties*
Fourth disobedience in whole test	*Elimination*
Fall of horse and/or rider	*30 penalties*
For every commenced second in excess of Time Allowed	*¼ penalty*
Exceeding Time Limit	*Elimination*
Knocking down a boundary flag	*2 penalties*

Dressage

Until there is a more thorough understanding in this country of the meaning of the word "Dressage" with regard to the training of the riding horse, there will be no marked improvement in the training of our hunters, hacks, polo ponies and children's ponies.

The word itself, being foreign, has proved somewhat of a stumbling block, but it is difficult to find a word in English to take its place. Dressage signifies the training of the horse for riding for pleasure as opposed to the training of the horse for the race-course, although the latter would, in all probability benefit if dressage were introduced into their early training as well. It would appear, therefore, that this word must be incorporated into the English language, in common with so many other French words such as "chauffeur", which signifies the driver of a private car as opposed to the driver of a lorry or bus.

It must be understood that a covered riding school or an open-air manège are not essentials. They are undoubtedly of great assistance, the former especially in the winter months, but as long as a flat piece of ground is available where the going is good and a fence along at least one side of it, to give direction, very excellent results can be obtained.

There is also a misconception which is prevalent among riding people, namely, that the object of dressage is to prepare horses for tests—that is entirely wrong. One does not learn to read and write in order to take part in examinations. Examinations have their use in testing the progress that is being made. It is the same with dressage tests, they are of value in ascertaining the progress that is being made in the training and in comparing the ability of one individual (horse or rider) against another.

The true purpose of dressage is to improve the standard of training of the riding horse and to provide a progressive system which will teach the horse to balance himself with the weight of his rider, without putting undue strain on any sets of joints or muscles, thus enabling him to comply easily and happily with the demands of his rider and to improve his paces and bearing.

The whole secret of dressage lies in placing the horse's head in the right position by controlling the hind legs. It is the rider's legs and seat that must be the chief influence in placing the horse's head, and a snaffle bridle is the only bit for the purpose. If an attempt is made to pull the horse's head into position with a double bridle, the mouth would inevitably be ruined and the action impaired. The double bridle should not be used until the position of the head is established.

The horse must be made to go forward by the hind legs propelling the fore legs immediately in front of them. He must be taught to increase and decrease his stride in all paces without altering the rhythm. He must be taught the lateral movements not only to enable him to go on two tracks, but in order to overcome evasions, to supple the spine, to teach the horse to be obedient to the rider's legs and to keep the horse straight.

The greatest difficulty in equitation is to keep the horse straight.

OBJECT and GENERAL PRINCIPLES

The object of Dressage is the harmonious development of the physique and ability of the horse. As a result, it makes the horse calm, supple and keen, thus achieving perfect understanding with its rider.

These qualities are revealed by:
the freedom and regularity of the paces;
the harmony, lightness and ease of the movements;
the lightening of the forehand and the engagement of the hind quarters;
the horse remaining absolutely straight in any movement along a straight line and bending accordingly when moving on curved lines.

The horse thus gives the impression of doing of his own accord what is required of him. Confident and attentive, he submits generously to the control of his rider.

His walk is regular, free and unconstrained. His trot is free, supple, regular, sustained and active. His canter is united, light and cadenced. His quarters are never inactive or sluggish. They respond to the slightest indication of the rider and thereby give life and spirit to all the rest of his body.

By virtue of a lively impulsion and the suppleness of his joints, free from the paralysing effects of resistance, the horse obeys willingly and without hesitation and responds to the various aids calmly and with precision.

In all his work, even at the halt, the horse must be on the bit. A horse is said to be "on the bit" when the hocks are correctly placed, the neck is more or less raised according to the extension or collection of the pace, the head remains steadily in position, the contact with the mouth is light and no resistance is offered to the rider.

The position of the horse when "on the bit" depends on the conformation as well as on the degree of training of the horse.

SPECIFIC REQUIREMENTS.

THE HALT. At the halt, the horse should stand attentive, motionless and straight, with the weight evenly distributed over all four legs, and be ready to move off at the slightest indication of the rider. The neck raised, the poll high, the head a little in front of the vertical, the mouth light, the horse champing his bit and maintaining a light contact with the rider's hand.

The transition from any pace to the halt should be made progressively in a smooth and precise movement.

THE WALK. The walk is a marching pace in which the four legs of the horse follow one another in four time, well marked and maintained in all work at the walk. When the four beats cease to be well marked, even and regular, the walk is disunited or broken.

It is at the pace of the walk that the imperfections in dressage are most marked. The pace will suffer if the degree of collection is not in accordance with the stage of schooling of the horse, but is precipitated.

The following walks are recognised: ordinary, collected, extended and free.

Ordinary walk. A free, regular and unconstrained walk of moderate extension. The horse should walk energetically but calmly, with even and determined steps, distinctly marking four equally-spaced beats. The rider should keep a light and steady contact with the mouth.

Herr Ottoker Pohlmann of Germany competes in the dressage class on Polarfuchs.

Collected walk. The horse moves resolutely forward, with his neck raised and arched. The head approaches the vertical position, the light contact with the mouth being maintained. The hind legs are engaged with good hock action. The pace should remain marching and vigorous, the legs being placed in regular sequence. Each step covers less ground and is higher than at the ordinary walk because all the joints bend more markedly. The hind feet touch the ground behind the footprints of the fore feet.

In order not to become hurried or irregular the collected walk is slightly shorter than the ordinary walk, although showing greater mobility.

Extended walk. The horse should cover as much ground as possible, without haste and without losing the regularity of his steps. The hind feet touch the ground clearly beyond the footprints of the fore feet. The rider lets the horse stretch out his head and neck without, however, losing contact, the head being carried in front of the vertical.

Free walk. The free walk is a pace of rest in which the reins being stretched to their utmost, the horse is allowed complete freedom of his head and neck.

THE TROT. The trot is a pace of two-time on alternate diagonals (near fore and off hind and vice-versa) separated by a moment of suspension.

The trot, always with free, active and regular steps, should be gone into without hesitation.

The quality of the trot is judged by the general impression, the elasticity and regularity of the steps and the impulsion, while maintaining the same cadence.

The following trots are recognised: ordinary, collected and extended.

Ordinary trot. This is a pace between the extended and the collected trot. The horse goes forward freely and straight, engaging his hind legs with good hock action, on a taut but light rein, his position being balanced and unconstrained. The steps should be as even as possible. The hind feet touch the ground in the footprints of the fore feet.

The degree of energy and impulsion displayed at the ordinary trot denotes clearly the degree of suppleness and balance of the horse.

The ordinary trot.

Collected trot. The neck is raised, thus enabling the shoulders to move with greater ease in all directions, the hocks being well engaged and maintaining energetic impulsion, notwithstanding the slower movement. The horse's steps are shorter but he is lighter and more mobile.

Extended trot. The horse covers as much ground as possible. He lengthens his stride, remaining on the bit with light contact. The neck is extended and, as a result of great impulsion from the quarters, the horse uses his shoulders, covering more ground at each step without his action becoming much higher.

The ordinary trot and extended trot are executed "rising" unless otherwise instructed. The collected trot is executed "sitting."

THE CANTER. The canter is a pace of three time. In the right canter for instance, the sequence is as follows, left hindleg, left diagonal (right hind and left foreleg), right foreleg followed by a period of suspension with all four legs in the air before taking the next stride.

The following canters are recognised: ordinary, collected and extended.

Ordinary canter. This is a pace between the extended canter and the collected canter. The horse, perfectly straight from head to tail, moves freely, with a natural balance. The strides are long, even and the pace well cadenced. The quarters develop an increasing impulsion at each stride.

Collected canter. At the collected canter, the shoulders are supple, free

Mrs. V. D. S. Williams demonstrates the extended trot on Little Model.

and mobile and the quarters very active. The horse's mobility is increased without any loss of impulsion.

Extended canter. The horse extends his neck; the tip of the nose points more or less forward, the horse lengthens his stride without losing any of his calmness and lightness.

134

COUNTER CANTER (FALSE CANTER). On the circle this is a suppling movement. The horse maintains his lateral flexion at the poll to the outside of the circle, in other words, remains bent to the leading leg. His conformation does not permit his spine to bend to the line of the circle.

The rider, avoiding any contortion, causing contraction and disorder, should especially endeavour to limit the deviation of the quarters to the outside and restrict his demands according to the degree of suppleness of the horse. (This movement is a canter to the left with the off fore leading, or to the right with the near fore leading.)

SIMPLE CHANGE OF LEG AT THE CANTER. This is a change whereby the horse is brought back into a walk and, after one or two well defined steps, restarted into a canter with the other leg leading.

THE CHANGE IN THE AIR. FLYING CHANGE OF LEG AT THE CANTER. The horse changes leg "in the air" in a single stride while cantering. This change of leg is termed as "flying" (or "in the air")

when it is executed at the moment of suspension which follows each stride at the canter. The horse remains straight, calm and light.

The ordinary canter

THE REIN BACK. The rein back is the walk backwards, the legs being raised and set down simultaneously by diagonal pairs. It is correct when the horse moves regularly in two time, the hind legs remaining well in line and the legs being well raised. The horse must be ready to halt or move forward without pausing at the demands of his rider, remaining at all times lightly on the bit and well balanced.

Any signs of hurrying, evasion of the hand, deviation of the quarters from the straight line or spreading and inactivity of the haunches are serious faults. Violent influence on the part of the rider may be detrimental to the joints of the hind quarters. A horse that is not obedient to the aids of the rider in the rein back is insufficiently suppled, badly schooled or badly ridden.

If, in a dressage test, a trot or a canter is required after a rein back, the horse must strike off immediately into this pace without an intermediate step.

SUBMISSION. At all paces, a slight flexion of the jaw, without nervousness, is a criterion of the obedience of the horse and of the harmonious distribution of his forces.

Grinding the teeth and swishing the tail are signs of resistance on the part of the horse. The judges must also take these into account in their marks for the general impression.

TRANSITIONS

CHANGE OF PACE AND SPEED. Such changes should always be quickly made, yet be smooth and not abrupt. The cadence of a pace should be maintained up to the moment when the pace or speed is changed or the horse halts. The horse remains light in hand, calm and maintains a correct position.

The same applies to transitions from the passage to the piaffer and from the piaffer to the passage.

CHANGES OF DIRECTION. At changes of direction, the horse should adjust the bend of his body to the curvature of the line he follows, remaining supple and following the indications of the rider without any resistance or change of pace or speed.

Counter-change of hand. The rider

Mr. L. Morgan (Australia) on Salad Days in dressage at Badminton.

changes direction by moving obliquely either to the quarter line or the centre line or to the opposite long side of the arena, whence he returns on an oblique line to the line he was following when he started the movement.

At the counter-change of hand the rider should make his horse straight an instant before changing direction.

When the number of steps to either side is prescribed in the schedule, it must be strictly observed and the movement be executed symmetrically.

Any abruptness while changing direction is faulty.

HALTS AND HALF-HALTS. The *halt* signifies the manner of stopping the horse at the end of a movement. Consequently, halt means "stop".

The halt is obtained by a displacement of the weight on to the quarters by the action of the seat and by a resisting action of the hand, causing an instantaneous stop, while the legs are kept in readiness to maintain the impulsion.

The *half-halt* is an action of the hand with the object of preparing for the full halt or the transition to a lesser pace. In shifting more weight on the quarters, the engagement of the hind legs and balance on the haunches are facilitated.

LATERAL WORK (WORK ON TWO TRACKS). The aim of the lateral movements is to bring the balance and the pace into harmony. They supple all parts of the horse, increasing especially the suppleness of the quarters and of the joints and the freedom of the shoulders. They also make the horse more obedient to the aids of the rider.

The lateral movements should only be practised for a short time and always be followed by some energetic movement straight forward.

At the lateral movements the horse is bent uniformly from the poll to the tail and moves with the forehand and the quarters on two distinct tracks. The distance between the tracks should not be more than one step. The pace remains always regular, supple and free, maintained by a constant impulsion; this is often lost because the rider is preoccupied with the bend of the horse only.

At the lateral movements the forehand should always be in advance of the quarters.

Lateral work comprises: the Shoulder-in, the Travers (Pass head to the wall), the Renvers (Pass tail to the wall), Pass diagonally across the arena and the Counter-Change of hand.

Shoulder-in. The horse is bent round the inside leg of the rider. The outside shoulder is placed in front of the inside hind quarter. The inside legs pass and cross in front of the outside legs. The horse's body is bent away from the direction to which he is moving.

The bend of the horse is more or less accentuated according to the degree of lateral suppleness the rider seeks to attain.

The horse should not be at an angle of more than 45° to the direction in which he is moving.

The shoulder-in is not a movement required in competitions or exhibitions but a schooling exercise, developing the obedience of the horse and the skill of the rider, at the same time being the foundation of the other lateral movements.

Travers. At the travers, the horse moves along the wall, being placed obliquely with the head to the wall at an angle of not more than 45°. The horse is bent very slightly round the inside leg of the rider and looks to the direction to which he is moving.

Renvers. The renvers is the inverse

position of the travers, with the tail instead of the head to the wall. Otherwise it is carried out following the same principles and conditions as at the travers, the horse looking in the direction to which he is moving.

Pass. The horse moves on two tracks, the head, neck and shoulders always slightly in advance of the quarters. A slight bend permitting the horse to look in the direction of the movement adds to his grace and gives more freedom of movement to the outside shoulder. The outside legs pass and cross in front of the inside legs. No slowing down of the pace is to be tolerated.

The legs on the side to which the horse is bent are the inside legs, those on the opposite side the outside legs.

The pass can be demanded on the diagonal across the arena, in which case the horse must remain parallel to the long side of the school.

In French, the Pass is termed "tenir les hanches", a term used in classical equestrian language to describe the actions of the rider causing his horse to move on two tracks.

At the counter-change of hands on two tracks (zig-zag) the attention of the judges should be concentrated on the changes of position of the horse, the movements of his legs and the precision, suppleness and regularity of his movements.

All bending or flexion at the poll has of necessity repercussion on the whole spine. Consequently, at all lateral movements the horse is bent to the direction in which he is looking. While this bend is hardly perceptible at the pass diagonally across the school, it is more evident in the travers, the renvers and the shoulder-in.

FIGURES

SERPENTINE. The first loop is started by moving gradually away from the short side and the last loop is finished by moving gradually towards the opposite short side.

FIGURE OF EIGHT. This is executed following the same rules as for the serpentine inside a square with X as the centre. The horse changes the bend at the centre of the eight through an absolutely straight position to be maintained for a length of a horse while passing from the one circle to the other.

PIROUETTES

HALF-PIROUETTE. This is the half-turn on the haunches. The forehand commences the half-turn, tracing a half-circle round the haunches, without pausing, at the moment the inside hind leg ceases its forward movement. The horse moves forward again, without a pause, upon completion of the half-turn.

During this movement the horse should maintain his impulsion and should never in the slightest move backwards or deviate sideways. It is necessary that the inside hind leg while forming the pivot should return to the same spot each time it leaves the ground.

PIROUETTE. This movement is a small circle on two tracks, with a radius equal to the length of the horse, the forehand moving round the haunches.

At whatever pace the pirouette is executed, the horse should turn smoothly, maintaining the exact cadence and sequence of legs at that pace.

At the pirouette, as at the half-

M. Michael Cochenet (France) on Hirondelle, competing in dressage at Harewood.

pirouette, the forelegs and the outside hind leg move round the inside hind leg, which forms the pivot and should return to the same spot each time it leaves the ground. If, at the canter, this leg is not raised and returned to the ground in the same way as the other hind leg, the pace is no longer regular.

In executing the pirouette, the rider should maintain perfect lightness while accentuating the collection and the engagement of the quarters.

The quality of the pirouette is appreciated according to the regularity of the pace, its suppleness and cadence, the unobtrusiveness of the rider's aids, and the position and contact of the horse during and after the execution of the movement.

Pirouettes and half-pirouettes can be carried out at all paces.

THE PASSAGE. This is a slow, shortened, very collected, very elevated and very cadenced trot. It is characterised by a pronounced engagement of the quarters, a more accentuated flexion of the knees and hocks and the graceful elasticity of the movement. Each diagonal pair of legs is raised and put to the ground alternately, gaining little ground and with an even cadence and a prolonged suspension.

In principle, the height of the toe of the raised foreleg should be level with the middle of the cannon bone of the other foreleg. The toe of the raised hind leg should be slightly above the fetlock joint of the other hind leg.

The neck should be raised and gracefully arched with the poll as the highest point and the head close to the perpendicular. The horse should remain light on the bit and be able to go smoothly from the passage into the piaffer and vice-versa, without apparent effort and without altering the cadence, the impulsion being always active and pronounced.

The same passage cannot be expected of all horses. Depending upon conformation and temperament, as well as the energy derived from the impulsion, some horses have a more rounded and longer action, others a more lively shorter action. Swinging the quarters from one side to the other is a fault.

THE PIAFFER. This movement is the collected trot on the spot. The horse's back is supple and vibrating. The haunches with active hocks are well engaged giving great freedom and lightness to the action of the shoulders and forelegs.

The neck is raised, the poll supple,

141

the head perpendicular, the mouth maintaining light contact on a taut rein. The alternate diagonals are raised with even, supple, cadenced and graceful movement, the moment of suspension being prolonged. In principle, the height of the toe of the raised foreleg should be level with the middle of the cannon bone of the other foreleg. The toe of the raised hind leg should be slightly lower, reaching just above the fetlock joint of the other hind leg.

The body of the horse should move up and down with a supple and harmonious movement without any swinging of either the forehand or the quarters from one side to the other.

The piaffer, although being executed strictly on the spot and with perfect balance, must always be animated by an energetic impulsion which is displayed in the horse's constant desire to move forward as soon as the aids calling for the piaffer are discontinued.

BRITISH HORSE SOCIETY'S DRESSAGE TESTS

CLASS E (ELEMENTARY).
Bridle: Ordinary snaffle or simple double bridle as may be specified. To be ridden with both hands.
Movements:

Walk—ordinary, free.
Trot—ordinary, extended.
Canter—ordinary, extended, simple changes of leg, counter canter (false canter).

Miss Sheila Wilcox on Airs and Graces.

142

Transitions—from any pace to any other pace, from a walk or trot into a halt and from a halt into a walk or trot.

Rein-back—a certain number of steps, not exceeding six.

Circles, half circles, changes of rein, including change through the circle, at all paces; serpentines.

Pirouettes at the walk.

CLASS M (MEDIUM).

Bridle: Simple double bridle.

To be ridden with both hands or with one hand if required for certain specified movements.

Movements: The following additional movements are included:

Walk—collected; on two tracks.

Trot—collected; on two tracks.

Canter—collected.

CLASS A (ADVANCED) (PRIX ST.-GEORGES).

Bridle: Simple double bridle.

To be ridden with both hands or with one hand if required for certain specified movements.

Movements: The following additional movements are included:

Canter on two tracks, change of leg in the air, including repeated changes down to every six, five, four or three strides; figures of eight at the true lead, and at the counter-lead with a change of leg in the air at the centre; figures of eight without a change of leg.

Pirouette or Half-Pirouette.

Horses in Class A shall not be required to jump.

CLASS O (OLYMPIC).

Bridle: Simple double bridle.

To be ridden with both hands or with one hand if required for certain specified movements.

Movements: The following additional movements are included:

Passage.

Piaffer.

Canter: change of leg every two strides and every stride.

Horses in Class O shall not be required to jump.

CHAPTER THIRTEEN

Brief History of Hunting

Foxhunting is the national sport of Great Britain and was looked upon by Mr. Beckford as an art. It may be considered to afford greater pleasure to all classes of society which are accustomed to participate in it than any other field sport. It is claimed that no one could define or state correctly the principle of sport, but nevertheless the allurements of the chase are stronger now than they have ever been, and attract larger fields of followers every year. Authorities differ with regard to the date in which foxhunting first became an amusement in England, but we may take it that it was not at all generally followed until the year 1756, though the Charlton, afterwards the Goodwood, were in existence in the reign of William III and the Bridgewater hounds, very soon afterwards, besides others. We read, indeed, that King James in the year 1603 was accustomed to hunt as a pastime in the course of the long journeys which were undertaken at that period. The followers and admirers of the Staintondale hounds in Yorkshire, claim for this pack that they were formed over 250 years ago. One of the earliest packs of foxhounds in the western part of England was established by Mr. Thomas Fowens, of Stapleton, in Dorsetshire about the year 1730. The Dukes of Beaufort and Rutland, the Earls of Yarborough and Fitzwilliam were amongst the earliest owners of celebrated packs, whose reputation has been jealously maintained ever since they were first established.

What is the objective to be obtained in the breeding of a pack of foxhounds today? Is it to show a fast burst to a hard riding field or is it to show a slow hound hunt to a lot of people who appreciate good hound work, or is it a combination of the above? It is important that hounds should kill foxes and farmers will not be satisfied unless they do. The long slow hunts of years ago are a thing of the past and today 80% of foxes killed are killed within 40 minutes of when they are found. This means the modern foxhound must be able to carry a good head on a decent scenting day and speed enough to push the quarry hard from the outset.

Let us suppose, then, that you have arrived at the Meet four or five minutes before the appointed hour. Don't be late or, if you are, don't blame the Master for having moved off without you. The Huntsman knows exactly where he is likely to find his first fox, stations his whippers-in as sentinels who will let him know when his quarry breaks. When the fox breaks he will be "halloaed away", and you or the rest of the field may see him go or you may not but the whipper-in's holloa followed by the Huntsman's cheer and the sound of his horn will denote that "the hunt is up" as they used to say in the olden days. Never jump unnecessarily. Remember

that the object is to get to the end of a hunt, which may be short or long, with the least possible effort on the part of your horse. If scent is good there should be no cause for the Master to caution you not to press hounds unduly but it may be after you have been galloping for ten minutes or so you will see the Master hold up his hand as a signal to the Field to "hold hard". Pull up and stand still. Hounds have checked, and until they can recover the line, with or without the aid of their huntsman, nothing should distract them. If hounds cannot recover the line by themselves, the huntsman will cast them ahead of him in a wide circle having as its centre the point at which they last spoke. Now you will see the reason which necessitated your pulling up instantly when you were signalled to do so. You will realise that a sweating horse gives off a smell which may well smother the less strong scent of a fox. Nothing annoys a huntsman more than to see the field moving about during a check.

We will suppose that hounds have recovered the line and have settled down to a real run and are running merrily over a good line of country with your horse going well and taking his fences as they come. Remember that although a fox can outrun his pursuers for the first few miles, even on the best scenting day, his staying powers are not as great as those of a fit foxhound, and that the time will come when he must have recourse to some of the astonishing subterfuges to better his pursuers, for which his race is famous. If you are watching hounds perhaps you will notice the leaders are faltering. Up will go the Master's hand again. Pull up your horse and watch, hounds may pursue the same tactics as before and fail. The huntsman will make his cast and presently the line is recovered and you are galloping behind the pack at a good steady pace. Ride a bit to one side, never ride directly behind hounds, because if they hear you coming, they will invariably almost stop and look back to avoid the danger which they fear may overtake them. Now the pace slackens, scent fails with a tired fox, and our quarry will begin to twist and turn in an effort to beat his pursuers. Now is the time to keep your eyes open, perhaps you will get a view of the hunted fox. What is that sneaking down the ditch underneath the fence—our fox surely. Don't holloa, it will only get hounds' heads up, hold your hat up, someone will see you, the Master has, he gallops up. "In the ditch" you say quietly, "dead beat". Here comes the Huntsman and you point to the exact spot where the quarry disappeared. Hounds hit off the line and very soon it is all over.

And so you hack quietly home and see that your horse, which has carried you so well, is comfortably put away for the night. See that he has plenty of clean straw, that he is warmly rugged up and has cleared up his feed. See to it, too, that the top door of his box is open and that he has plenty of fresh air. Then sit down in front of the fire and tell your friend, who was not out, how well hounds hunted and how well you went!

GLOSSARY OF HUNTING TERMS

"All on". Term used by the Whipper-in to indicate that every hound is up with the pack.

Appointment Card. The card of forthcoming events giving dates and places.

"As Hounds ran". The distance covered by hounds in a run measuring each turn as opposed to "as the crow flies".

"At Fault". Term indicating that hounds have lost the line.

Babbler. A hound which throws its tongue too much especially when far behind the others.

Bag-fox. A fox set loose for hunting.

Beagles. Small hounds for hunting hares.

Blooded. A hunt ceremony when young riders are at their first kill.

Bolt a Fox. To force a fox out of a drain or earth.

Bottom. Term indicating an unjumpable deep ditch or brook.

Brace. Two foxes. One fox = ½ brace: 2½ brace = 5 foxes.

Break. A fox "breaks" when it leaves covert.

Break-up. When hounds eat the carcase of the hunted fox.

Brush. The tail of a fox.

Bullfinch. A thick high fence the top part of which must be pushed through.

Cap. The fee paid by Visitors for a day's hunting.

"Carrying a Scent". A good scenting country.

Cast. An effort made by the Huntsman to get hounds back on to the line.

Chop. When hounds kill a fox very quickly without a chase.

Country. Term indicating the country over which any pack may hunt.

Couple. Two hounds—a single hound is known as "one hound", more than one as so many couple.

Couples. Hound Collars carried on the saddle of the Hunt Staff.

Course. To run a fox into view.

Covert. Term indicating a small wood (woodland).

Cry. The sound made by the pack when actually hunting a fox or a hare.

Cub. A young fox.

Cub-Hunting. Introducing young hounds to hunting and encouraging fox cubs to leave covert.

Cur-dog. A term in Hunting for any dog other than a hound.

Dog Fox. A male fox.

Drag-hunt. Using an artificial scent or drag when hunting with a pack of hounds.

Draw. The area which the Huntsman will draw looking for a fox.

Earth. The underground home of a fox.

147

Earth Stopper. On the night previous to a hunt the entrance to an earth is blocked by an earth stopper when the fox is out.

Feather. When a hound is uncertain and does not speak to the line but "feathers" by driving along the presumed line with its nose to the ground.

Field. A term indicating all the mounted followers.

Field Master. The Master or someone appointed by him to control the Field.

Flags. A kennel term indicating the bricks or stone floor of the kennel yards.

Flesh. A kennel term for the meat on which hounds are fed.

Fresh Fox. When hounds change from the hunted fox to another.

Gone to Ground. When a fox has gone into an earth or drain.

Harriers. A pack of hounds for hunting hares.

Heads up. Hounds which have lost the line get their heads up.

Heel. When hounds run the fox in the opposite direction.

Hoick Holloa! A cheer calling hounds to a Holloa.

Hold up. To prevent foxes leaving a covert.

Horn. Usually made of copper with a nickel or silver mouth piece.

Hunt Servants. Huntsman, (if professional) Kennel Huntsman and Whippers-in.

Kennels. A collective term for the various buildings and yards where the pack lives.

Lawn Meet. An invitation Meet at a private house.

M.F.H. Master of Foxhounds.

M.H. Master of Hounds, whether Stag, Harriers, Beagles, Basset, Drag or other.

Mark to ground. When hounds bay outside an earth or drain.

Mask. A fox's head.

Meet. The place appointed for a pack to meet on a hunting day.

Music. The cry of hounds when hunting.

Opening Meet. The first Meet of the regular season.

Pad. The foot of a fox.

Point. The point of a run is the distance "as the crow flies".

Rate, To. To rebuke or scold a hound.

Riot. When hounds hunt any other animal than their proper quarry.

Scent is given off by glands of a hunted animal and enables hounds to follow it.

Scut. The tail of a hare.

Slot. The foot or footprint of a deer.

Speak. Hounds "speak" rather than "bark".

Stag. A male deer at 4 years of age and over.

Stale Line. The line of a fox which has been passed previously.

Stern. A hound's tail.

Tail Hounds. Hounds which are some way behind the main pack when running.

Tongue. "Giving tongue", the cry of hounds when hunting.

Trencher-fed. Hounds not kept in kennel but looked after by Members of the Hunt.

Unentered. A hound which has not completed a Cub-hunting Season.

Vixen. A female fox.

Whipper-in. Huntsman's Assistant.

Young Entry. Young hounds before Cub-hunting.

CHAPTER FOURTEEN

Hunt List

FOXHOUNDS— ENGLAND and WALES

ALBRIGHTON. *Country* Staffordshire and Shropshire: *Kennels* Whiston Cross, Albrighton, Wolverhampton, Staffs. *Meet* Tues., Thurs., Sat.

ALBRIGHTON WOODLAND. *Country* between Birmingham, Bromsgrove, Bewdley, Bridgnorth and Wolverhampton main roads: *Kennels* Hurcott nr. Kidderminster, Worcs. *Meet* Wed. and Sat.

Meet of the Albrighton Woodland Hunt.

ASHFORD VALLEY. *Country* Weald of Kent—Ashford, Tenterden, Headcorn district: *Kennels* The Forest, Hothfield nr. Ashford, Kent. *Meet* Mon. or Wed., and Sat.

ATHERSTONE. *Country* West Leicestershire and North Warwickshire: *Kennels* Witherley, Atherstone, Warwickshire. *Meet* Tues., Wed., Fri. and Sat.

AVON VALE. *Country* Wiltshire round Melksham, Chippenham and Calne: *Kennels* Spye Park, Chippenham, Wilts. *Meet* Tues. and Sat.

BADSWORTH. *Country* Adjoins Grove, Bramham Moor, Holderness and York and Ainsty: *Kennels* Hillthorpe, East Hardwick, Yorks. *Meet* Tues. and Sat., occ. Thurs.

BANWELL. *Country* Leased from Mendip Farmers and consists of a strip from Bristol to Bridgwater: *Kennels* Pool Farm, Wolvershill, Banwell, Somerset. *Meet* 2 days a week.

BARLOW. *Country* N. E. Derbyshire: *Kennels* Holmesfield, Sheffield, Yorks. *Meet* Mon. and Sat.

BEAUFORT'S, DUKE OF. *Country* Gloucestershire, Somerset and Wiltshire: *Kennels* Badminton, Glos. *Meet* 4 days a week.

BEDALE. *Country* North Riding of Yorkshire: *Kennels* Low Street, Northallerton, Yorks. *Meet* alt. Mon., Fri. and Mon., Wed. and Fri.

BELVOIR. *Country* Leicestershire and Lincolnshire: *Kennels* Belvoir Castle, Lincs. *Meet* Tues., Wed., Fri. and Sat.

BERKELEY'S, EARL OF. *Country* adjoining Cotswold and Ledbury and in the East the Beaufort: *Kennels* Berkeley, Glos. *Meet* 3 days a week.

BERKELEY, OLD. *Country* Hertfordshire and Buckinghamshire: *Kennels* Kimblewick, Aylesbury, Bucks. *Meet* alt. Tues. and Sat. and Tues., Thurs., Sat.

BERKSHIRE, OLD. *Country* Berkshire and Oxfordshire: *Kennels* Farringdon, Berks. *Meet* Mon., Wed. and Sat.

BERKS., SOUTH. *Country* Berkshire and Oxfordshire: *Kennels* Goddard's Green, Mortimer, Berks. *Meet* Wed. and Sat.

BEWCASTLE. *Country* Borders of Scotland, Northumberland and Cumberland: *Kennels* Ainstable, Carlisle, Cumberland. *Meet* Mon., Thurs. and Sat.

BICESTER AND WARDEN HILL. *Country* Oxfordshire, Buckinghamshire and Northamptonshire: *Kennels* Stratton

AUDLEY, Oxon. *Meet* Mon., Tues., Thurs. and Sat.

BILSDALE. *Country* Yorkshire around Thirsk, Stokesley and Hemsley: *Kennels* Hill End, Bilsdale, Yorks. *Meet* Tues. and Sat.

BISLEY (FULTON'S). *Country* Surrey: *Kennels* Chaseley, Bisley, Surrey. *Meet* Sat.

BLACKMORE VALE. *Country* Dorset and Somerset: *Kennels* Charlton Hawthorne, Sherborne, Dorset. *Meet* Tues., Wed., Fri. and Sat.

BLANKNEY. *Country* Lincolnshire and Notts. *Kennels* Blankney, Lincs. *Meet* Wed. and Sat.

BLENCATHRA. *Country* Lake District: *Kennels* Gate, Ghyll, Threlkeld, Cumberland. *Meet* 3 days a week. A foot pack.

BORDER. *Country* N.W. Northumberland and Roxburghshire: *Kennels* Overacres Farm, Otterburn, Northumberland. *Meet* 5 days a fortnight.

BRAES OF DERWENT. *Country* S. Northumberland and N.W. Durham: *Kennels* Timbler Hill, Shotley Bridge, Northumberland. *Meet* Wed. and Sat.

BRAMHAM MOOR. *Country* West Riding of Yorkshire: *Kennels* Hope Hall, Bramham, Boston Spa, Yorks. *Meet* Wed. and Sat., alt. Mon.

BRECON. *Country* between Brecon Beacons and the River Wye: *Kennels* Canal Bank, Brecon. *Meet* Wed. and Sat.

BROCKLESBY. *Country* Lincolnshire: *Kennels* Brocklesby, Harbrough, Lincs. *Meet* Wed. and Sat.

BURGHLEY. *Country* Lincolnshire: *Kennels* Burghley House, Stamford, Lincs. *Meet* Wed. and Sat.

BURTON. *Country* bounded to the South by the Blankney, to the North by the Brocklesby, to the West by the Grove and Rufford and to the East by the Southwold. *Kennels* Riseholm, Lincoln. *Meet* Wed. and Sat.

CAMBRIDGESHIRE. *Country* Cambridgeshire, Huntingdonshire and Bedfordshire: *Kennels* Caxton, Cambs. *Meet* Tues. and Fri.

CARMARTHENSHIRE. *Country* about 15 miles around Carmarthen. *Kennels* Castel Gorford, St. Clears, Carmarthen. *Meet* Mon. and Thurs.

CATTISTOCK. *Country* Dorset and S. Somerset: *Kennels* Cattistock, Dorset. *Meet* 4 days a week.

151

CHESHIRE. *Country* Cheshire (less Wirral): *Kennels* Sandiway, Cheshire. *Meet* Mon., Wed. and Sat.

CHESHIRE FOREST. *Country* The Wirral peninsula: *Kennels* Littleton Old Hall, nr. Chester. *Meet* Tues., Thurs. and Sat.

CHIDDINGFOLD AND LECONFIELD. *Country* Surrey and Sussex: *Kennels* Petworth, Sussex. *Meet* Mon., Wed. and Sat.

CHIDDINGFOLD FARMERS'. *Country* The Surrey Hills: *Kennels* Enstead Gardens, Godalming, Surrey. *Meet* Wed. and Sat.

CLEVELAND. *Country* North Riding of Yorkshire: *Kennels* Tocketts, Guisborough, Yorks. *Meet* 3 days a week.

CLIFTON-ON-TEME. *Country* loaned by the Worcestershire, North Hereford and Ludlow Hunts: *Kennels* Tadstone, nr. Bromyard, Herefordshire. *Meet* Wed. and Sat.

COLLEGE VALLEY. *Country* loaned by the Duke of Buccleuch's, North Northumberland and Border Hunts: *Kennels* Langham Toll, Kilham, Mindrum, Northumberland. *Meet* Tues., Thurs. and Sat.

CONISTON. *Country* Westmorland and Lancashire: *Kennels* Greenbank, Ambleside, Westmorland. *Meet* 3 days a week. A foot pack.

CORNWALL, EAST. *Country* Cornwall: *Kennels* Little Gimble, St. Clear, Cornwall. *Meet* Tues. and Fri.

CORNWALL, NORTH. *Country* Cornwall: *Kennels* St. Berward, North Cornwall. *Meet* 2 days a week.

COTSWOLD. *Country* Gloucestershire: *Kennels* Andoversford, Gloucestershire. *Meet* Mon., Wed. and Sat.

COTSWOLD, NORTH. *Country* Gloucestershire and Worcestershire: *Kennels* Broadway, Worcs. *Meet* Mon., Wed. and Sat.

COTSWOLD VALE FARMERS'. *Country* the Cotswold Vale and the Newent area. *Kennels* Boddington Manor, Cheltenham. *Meet* Tues. and Fri.

COTTESMORE. *Country* Rutland, Leicestershire and Lincolnshire: *Kennels* Ashwell, Oakham, Rutland. *Meet* Tues., Thurs. and Sat.

COWDRAY. *Country* West Sussex. *Kennels* Balls Farm, Cowdray Park, Midhurst, Sussex. *Meet* Tues. and Sat.

CRAVEN FARMERS'. *Country* Berkshire, Hampshire and Wiltshire: *Kennels* Baydon House Farm, Baydon, Berks. *Meet* Wed. and Sat.

CRAWLEY AND HORSHAM. *Country* Sussex: *Kennels* West Grinstead, Horsham, Sussex. *Meet* Tues., Thurs. and Sat.

CROOME. *Country* Worcestershire, Warwickshire and Gloucestershire. *Kennels* Kinnersley, Severn Stoke, Worcester: *Meet* Tues. and Sat.

CUMBERLAND. *Country* Cumberland: *Kennels* Brayton, Aspatria, Cumberland. *Meet* Mon. and Thurs.

CUMBERLAND FARMERS'. *Country* between Penrith Castle and Wigton: *Kennels* Walton, Carlisle, Cumberland. *Meet* Wed. and Sat.

CURRE. *Country* between Usk and Chepstow: *Kennels* Ilton, Chepstow, Mon. *Meet* Tues. and Sat.

DARTMOOR. *Country* Devon: *Kennels* Ivybridge, S. Devon. *Meet* Tues., Wed., Fri. and Sat.

DAVID DAVIES. *Country* Central Montgomeryshire: *Kennels* Llandinian, Montgomery. *Meet* Sat. and byes.

DERWENT. *Country* North Riding of Yorkshire: *Kennels* Snainton, Yorks. *Meet* Tues. and Sat.

DEVON, EAST. *Country* S. E. Devon: *Kennels* Clyst St. Mary, nr. Exeter, Devon. *Meet* Tues. and Sat., alt. Thurs.

DEVON, MID. *Country* Dartmoor District: *Kennels* Factory Cross, Chagford, Devon. *Meet* Tues. and Sat.

DEVON, SOUTH. *Country* S. Devon: *Kennels* Pulsford, nr. Denbury, Newton Abbot, Devon. *Meet* Mon., Tues., Thurs. and Sat.

DORSET, SOUTH. *Country* Dorset: *Kennels* Bere Regis, Wareham, Dorset. *Meet* Mon., Thurs. and Sat.

DULVERTON, EAST. *Country* Edge of Exmoor: *Kennels* East Anstey, Tiverton, Devon. *Meet* 2 days a week.

DULVERTON, WEST. *Country* N. Devon and W. Somerset: *Kennels* Court Hall, North Molton, Devon. *Meet* Mon., Wed. and Fri.

DURHAM, SOUTH. *Country* Co. Durham: *Kennels* Hardwick Park, Sedgefield, Durham. *Meet* alt. Tues. and Wed.—Sat.

EGGESFORD. *Country* Devon: *Kennels* Wembworthy, N. Devon. *Meet* Mon., Thurs., Sat.

ENFIELD CHACE. *Country* Hertfordshire and Middlesex: *Kennels* Holiwell Court,

ESSENDON, Herts. *Meet* Tues. and Sat.

ERIDGE. *Country* South of Tunbridge Wells: *Kennels* Hamsel, Tunbridge Wells, Kent. *Meet* Wed. and Sat.

ESKDALE AND ENNERDALE. *Country* Cumberland, Westmorland and Lancashire: *Kennels* Sword House, Eskdale, Cumberland. *Meet* 3 days a week.

ESSEX. *Country* Essex: *Kennels* Harlow, Essex. *Meet* Mon., Wed., Sat.

ESSEX, EAST. *Country* N.W. and E. Essex: *Kennels* Earls Colne, Essex. *Meet* Tues., Thurs., Sat.

ESSEX FARMERS'. *Country* between the East Essex and the Essex Union: *Kennels* Althorne Lodge, Althorne, nr. Burnham-on-Crouch, Essex. *Meet* Sat., alt. Wed.

ESSEX UNION. *Country* S.E. Essex: *Kennels* Billericay, Essex. *Meet* Tues., Thurs., Sat.

ESSEX AND SUFFOLK. *Country* partly in Essex and partly in Suffolk (both sides of the River Stour). *Kennels* Layham, nr. Hadleigh, Suffolk. *Meet* Mon., Wed., Thurs., Sat.

EXMOOR. *Country* Devon and Somerset: *Kennels* Balewater, Simonsbath, Minehead, Somerset. *Meet* 5 days a fortnight.

FARNDALE. *Country* N. Yorkshire: *Kennels* Hall Farm, Farndale, Yorkshire. *Meet* Tues. and Sat.

FERNIE. *Country* S. Leicestershire: *Kennels* Great Bowden, Lincs. *Meet* Wed. and Sat.

FITZWILLIAM (MILTON). *Country* Northants. and Hunts.: *Kennels* Milton, nr. Peterborough, Northants. *Meet* Mon., Wed., Sat.

FLINT AND DENBIGH. *Country* Western parts of Flintshire and Denbighshire. *Kennels* Cefu, St. Asaph, Flintshire. *Meet* Tues. and Sat.

FOUR BURROW. *Country* Cornwall: *Kennels* Scorrier, Cornwall. *Meet* 3 days a week.

GARTH. *Country* Berkshire and Hampshire: *Kennels* Bracknell, Berks. *Meet* Mon. and Fri., occ. Sat.

GELLIGAER FARMERS'. *Country* N.E. Glamorgan and parts of Monmouthshire: *Kennels* Summerfield Hall, Maesycwmmer, Glam. *Meet* Sat. Alt. Wed.

GLAISDALE. *Country* North Riding of Yorkshire: *Kennels* Fryup Hall, Lealholm, Yorks. *Meet* Tues. and Sat.

GLAMORGAN. *Country* Vale of Glamorgan: *Kennels* Penllyn Castle, Cowbridge, Glam. *Meet* Mon. and Thurs.

GOATHLAND. *Country* Each side of the river Esk: *Kennels* Eskdaleside, Sleights, Yorks. *Meet* Tues. and Fri.

GOGGERDAN. *Country* N. Cardiganshire: *Kennels* Ffynnon Caradog, Aberystwyth. *Meet* Wed. and Sat.

GOLDEN VALLEY. *Country* Hereford, Radnor and Brecon: *Kennels* Whitney-on-Wye, Hereford. *Meet* Tues. and Sat.

GRAFTON. *Country* S. Northants. and N. Bucks. *Kennels* Paulerspury, Towcester. *Meet* Tues., Thurs. and Sat.

GROVE AND RUFFORD. *Country* Notts., Yorks. and Derbyshire: *Kennels* Barnby Moor, Retford, Notts. *Meet* Tues., Thurs., Sat.

HAMBLEDON. *Country* Hants.: *Kennels* Droxford, Hants. *Meet* Wed., Sat., alt. Mon.

HAMPSHIRE (H.H.). *Country* Hants.: *Kennels* Ropley, Alresford, Hants. *Meet* Mon., Tues., Thurs., Sat.

HAYDON. *Country* S.W. Northumberland. *Kennels* Langley Castle, Haydon Bridge, Northumberland. *Meet* Wed. and Sat.

HEREFORDSHIRE, NORTH. *Country* N.

HEREFORDSHIRE: *Kennels* Bodenham, Hereford. *Meet* Tues. and Sat.

HEREFORDSHIRE, SOUTH. *Country* S. Herefordshire: *Kennels* Wormslow, Hereford. *Meet* Tues. and Sat., occ. Thurs.

HERTFORDSHIRE. *Country* Herts. and Beds.: *Kennels* Houghton Regis, Dunstable, Beds. *Meet* Mon., Wed., Sat.

HEYTHROP. *Country* Oxfordshire and Gloucestershire: *Kennels* Chipping Norton, Oxon. *Meet* Mon., Wed., Fri. and Sat.

HOLDERNESS. *Country* East Riding of Yorks.: *Kennels* Elton, Brierley, Yorks. *Meet* Tues. and Sat.

HURSLEY. *Country* Hants.: *Kennels* Braishfield, Romsey, Hants. *Meet* Tues., Fri., occ. Sat.

HURWORTH. *Country* N. Yorks. and S. Durham: *Kennels* West Rounton, Northallerton, Yorks. *Meet* 2 days a week.

IRFON AND TOWY. *Country* Borders of Breconshire and Carmarthenshire. *Kennels* Glynsaer, Cynghordy, Llandovery. *Meet* Various.

ISLE OF WIGHT. *Country* The Isle of Wight: *Kennels* Gatcombe, Newport, I.O.W. *Meet* Wed. and Sat.

KENT, EAST. *Country* E. Kent: *Kennels* Eltham, nr. Canterbury, Kent. *Meet* Wed. and Sat.

KENT, WEST. *Country* W. Kent: *Kennels* Hamptons, Shipbourne, nr. Tonbridge, Kent. *Meet* 2 days a week.

LAMERTON. *Country* W. Devon and N.E. Cornwall: *Kennels* Stowford, Endown, Okehampton, Devon. *Meet* Mon. and Thurs.

LEDBURY. *Country* Hereford, Worcester and Gloucester: *Kennels* Bromesbarrow, Ledbury. *Meet* Mon., Fri., occ. Wed.

LEDBURY, NORTH. *Country* loaned by the Ledbury and mainly the Northern part. *Kennels* Suckley, Worcester. *Meet* Sat. and occ. bye.

LEWES'S. *Country* Mid-Cardiganshire: *Kennels* Llanyron, Cilian Arron, Lampeter, Cardigan. *Meet* Tues. and Fri.

LLANDILO FARMERS'. *Country* Carmarthenshire: *Kennels* Pantyrodyn, Capel Isaac, Llandilo, Carmarthen. *Meet* Tues., alt. Fri. and Sat.

LLANGEINOR. *Country* Glamorgan: *Kennels* Derwen Goppa, Coity, nr. Bridgend, Glam. *Meet* Wed. and Sat.

LLANGIBBY. *Country* Monmouthshire: *Kennels* Llangibby, Mon. *Meet* Tues. and Sat.

LONSDALE, NORTH. *Country* That part of North Lonsdale not hunted by the Coniston Foxhounds: *Kennels* Pennybridge Hall, Ulverston, Lancs. *Meet* 3 days a week. A foot pack.

LUDLOW. *Country* Shropshire, Herefordshire and Worcestershire: *Kennels* Coynham, Ludlow, Salop. *Meet* Mon., Wed., Sat.

LUNESDALE. *Country* Westmorland, West Riding of Yorkshire and N. Lancashire: *Kennels* New House, Orton, Westmorland. *Meet* 3 days a week. A foot pack.

MELBREAK. *Country* W. Cumberland: *Kennels* Miller Place, Lorton, Cockermouth. *Meet* Mon., Thurs., Sat.

MENDIP FARMERS'. *Country* Adjoins Beaufort in the North, Blackmore Dale in the South, South and West Wilts. and Avon Vale in the East. *Kennels* Priddy nr. Wells, Som. *Meet* Wed. and Sat.

MEYNELL. *Country* Derbyshire and Staffordshire: *Kennels* Sudbury, Derbyshire. *Meet* Tues., Sat., occ. Thurs.

MIDDLETON AND MIDDLETON EAST. *Country* North and East Ridings of Yorkshire. *Kennels* Birdsall, Malton,

Yorks. *Meet* Mon., Wed., Fri. and Sat.
MILVAIN (PERCY). *Country* Northumberland. *Kennels* Belford, Northumberland. *Meet* Tues., Thurs., Sat.—Mon. and Fri. every 3rd week.

MONMOUTHSHIRE. *Country* Northern half of Monmouthsire: *Kennels* Gobion, Abergavenny. *Meet* Wed. and Sat., occ. Mon.

MORPETH. *Country* South Northumberland. *Kennels* Rivergreen, Morpeth, Northumberland. *Meet* Tues., Sat., alt. Thurs.

NEW FOREST. *Country* Mainly in the New Forest: *Kennels* Furzey Lawn, Lyndhurst, Hants. *Meet* Tues. and Sat.

NEWMARKET AND THURLOW. *Country* between Cambridgeshire and Suffolk: *Kennels* Thurlow, Suffolk. *Meet* Mon., Thurs.

NORFOLK, WEST. *Country* Norfolk: *Kennels* Corbett's Lodge, Necton, King's Lynn, Norfolk. *Meet* Mon., Wed., Sat., occ. Thurs.

NORTHUMBERLAND, NORTH. *Country* N. Northumberland. *Kennels* Slainsfield, Cornhill-on-Tweed, Northumberland: *Meet* Mon., Fri., occ. Wed.

NOTTS., SOUTH. *Country* Nottinghamshire and Derbyshire: *Kennels* Epperstour, Notts. *Meet* Mon. and Thurs.

OAKLEY. *Country* Beds., Bucks., Northants. and Hunts. *Kennels* Milton Ernest, Bedford. *Meet* Tues., Thurs., Sat.

The Oakley Foxhounds.

OXFORDSHIRE, SOUTH. *Country* Oxfordshire: *Kennels* Stadhampton, Oxon. *Meet* Tues., Sat. and at least 1 Thurs. per month.

PANDY. *Country* N. Mon. and S. Hereford: *Kennels* Little Park, Llanvihangel-Crucorney, Abergavenny, Mon. *Meet* Wed. and Sat.

PEMBROKESHIRE. *Country* Pembrokeshire North of Milford Haven: *Kennels* Slade, Haverfordwest, Pembroke. *Meet* Wed. and Sat.

PEMBROKESHIRE, SOUTH. *Country* S. Pembrokeshire and a little of Carmarthenshire. *Kennels* Cressally, Kilgetly, Pembrokeshire. *Meet* Wed. and Sat.

PENNINE, SOUTH. *Country* The Pennine Hills in the West Riding and East Lancashire: *Kennels* Crow Point, Boothtown, Halifax, Yorks. *Meet* Sat. and byes. A foot pack.

PENTYRCH. *Country* Between Cardiff and Pontypridd, each side of the river Taff. *Kennels* Pentyrch, Glamorgan. *Meet* Tues. and Sat.

PERCY. *Country* Northumberland: *Kennels* Candigate, Alnwick, Northd. *Meet* Tues. and Sat.

PERCY, WEST. *Country* Lent by the Duke of Northumberland, bounded by Milvain in the North, Percy in the East, Morpeth in the South and Border in the West: *Kennels* Callaly High House, Whittingham, Northumberland. *Meet* Tues. and Sat.

PLAS MACHYNLLETH. *Country* The hilly countryside within a six mile radius of Machynlleth: *Kennels* Machynlleth, Montgomeryshire. *Meet* 5 days a fortnight. A foot pack.

PORTMAN. *Country* Dorset: *Kennels* Bryanston, nr. Blandford, Dorset. *Meet* Mon., Wed., alt. Fri. and Sat.

PUCKERIDGE. *Country* E. Herts. and W. Essex: *Kennels* Brent Pelham, Buntingford, Herts. *Meet* Wed., Sat., occ. Mon.

PYTCHLEY. *Country* Northants. and Leicestershire. *Kennels* Brixworth, Northampton. *Meet* Mon., Wed. and Sat.

PYTCHLEY, WOODLAND. *Country* Northamptonshire: *Kennels* Brigstock, Northants. *Meet* Wed. and Sat.

QUORN. *Country* Leicestershire: *Kennels* Barrow-on-Sour, Loughborough, Leics. *Meet* Mon., Tues., Fri. and Sat.

RADNORSHIRE AND WEST HEREFORDSHIRE. *Country* N.W. Herefordshire and a part of Radnorshire. *Kennels* Titby, Kington, Hereford. *Meet* Mon. and Fri.

ROMNEY MARSH. *Country* E. Sussex and Kent: *Kennels* Iden, Sussex. *Meet* 2 days a week.

R.A. (SALISBURY PLAIN). *Country* South portion of the Tedworth country loaned by that Hunt. *Kennels* Bulford Camp, Salisbury. *Meet* Wed. and Sat.

SALTERSGATE FARMERS'. *Country* N. Yorks. *Kennels* Lockton, Yorks. *Meet* Mon. and Sat.

SANDHURST. *Country* Roughly an 8-mile radius of Camberley, loaned by the Garth Hunt. *Kennels* Staff College, Camberley, Surrey. *Meet* Wed. and Sat.

SEAVINGTON. *Country* Dorset and Somerset: *Kennels* Seavington St. Mary, Ilminster, Som. *Meet* Mon., Thurs., Sat.

SENNYBRIDGE AND DISTRICT FARMERS'. *Country* About a 5-mile radius from Sennybridge: *Kennels* Sennybridge, Brecon. *Meet* Tues. and Sat.

SHROPSHIRE, NORTH. *Country* Shropshire: *Kennels* Lee Bridge, Preston Brockhurst, Salop. *Meet* Wed., Sat., occ. bye.

SHROPSHIRE, SOUTH. *Country* A radius 10 miles south of Shrewsbury. *Kennels* Annscroft, Salop. *Meet* Mon., Thurs., occ. Sat.

SILVERTON. *Country* Devonshire: *Kennels* Dreens Clieve, Stoke Hill, Exeter. *Meet* Wed. and Sat.

SINNINGTON. *Country* North Riding of Yorkshire: *Kennels* Kirby Moorside, Yorks. *Meet* Mon. and Thurs.

SOMERSET, WEST. *Country* Somerset including the Brandon Hills: *Kennels* Bowerhayes, Carhampton, nr. Minehead, Som. *Meet* Wed. and Sat.

SOMERSET VALE, WEST. *Country* Somerset including the Quantock Hills: *Kennels* Swang, Cannington, Bridgwater, Som. *Meet* Tues., Fri., occ. Sat.

SOUTHDOWN. *Country* Sussex Seaboard. *Kennels* Ringmer, Sussex. *Meet* Mon., Wed., Sat.

SOUTH WOLD. *Country* Lincolnshire: *Kennels* Belchford, Horncastle. *Meet* Tues., Sat.

SPOONERS. *Country* A 12-mile radius of Tavistock: *Kennels* Mason's Gate, Sampford Spinney, Tavistock. *Meet* Tues. and Sat.

STAFFORDSHIRE, NORTH. *Country* North of Stafford and bordering Shropshire, Cheshire and Derbyshire: *Kennels* Hill Chorlton, Baldwins Gate, nr. Newcastle, Staffs. *Meet* Tues. and Sat.

STAFFORDSHIRE, SOUTH. *Country* Staffordshire and Warwickshire: *Kennels* Upper Longdon, Rugeley, Staffs. *Meet* Tues. and Sat.

STEVENSTONE. *Country* N. Devon. *Kennels* The Old Kennels, Torrington, Devon. *Meet* Mon., Wed., Fri., Sat.

SUFFOLK. *Country* W. Suffolk. *Kennels* Borton Road, Bury St. Edmunds, Suffolk. *Meet* Tues. and Sat.

SURREY, OLD, AND BURSTOW. *Country* Surrey, Sussex and Kent: *Kennels* Felbridge, East Grinstead, Sussex. *Meet* Mon., Wed. and Sat.

SURREY UNION. *Country* Bounded in the North by the North Downs, in the East by the Brighton railway line; in the South, Three Bridges to Horsham and in the West by the Horsham-Guildford Road: *Kennels* Oakwood Hill, Ockley, Surrey. *Meet* Wed. and Sat.

SUSSEX, EAST. *Country* E. Sussex: *Kennels* Catsfield, Sussex. *Meet* Tues. and Sat.

TAUNTON VALE. *Country* Somerset: *Kennels* Henlade, Taunton, Som. *Meet* Tues., Fri.; Mon., Wed., Fri. alt.

TEDWORTH. *Country* Wilts. and Hants. *Kennels* Westcourt, Burbage, Marlborough, Wilts. *Meet* Tues. and Sat.

TEME VALLEY. *Country* Radnorshire, Herefordshire and Shropshire: *Kennels* Knighton, Radnorshire. *Meet* Tues. and Sat.

Parading the hounds of the South Staffordshire Hunt.

STAINTONDALE. *Country* Between Scarborough and Whitby, Yorks.: *Kennels* Stainton Farm, Staintondale, Scarborough, Yorks. *Meet* Tues. and Fri.

TETCOTT. *Country* Devon and Cornwall: *Kennels* Weekstone, Holsworthy, Devon. *Meet* Mon. and Thurs.

TETCOTT, SOUTH. *Country* Borders of Devon and Cornwall: *Kennels* Tetcott, Holsworthy, Devon. *Meet* Tues. and Sat.

THANET AND HERNE. *Country* Between the Canterbury-Whitstable road and the River Stour: *Kennels* Highstead, Gravel Pit, Chislet, nr. Canterbury. *Meet* Sat., occ. bye.

TICKHAM. *Country* Kent: *Kennels* Wren's Hill, nr. Faversham, Kent. *Meet* Wed. and Sat.

TIVERTON. *Country* Devon and small part of West Somerset: *Kennels* Hensleigh, Tiverton, Devon. *Meet* Wed. and Sat.

TIVYSIDE. *Country* S. Cardiganshire and N. Pembrokeshire: *Kennels* Felin Nart, Boncath, Pembrokeshire. *Meet* Tues., Thurs., Sat.

TORRINGTON FARMERS'. *Country* Loaned by Stevenstone Foxhounds and lies east of the River Torridge: *Kennels* Stevenstone, St. Giles, Torrington, Devon. *Meet* Mon., Wed., Sat.

TOWI AND COTHI. *Country* N. Carmarthenshire: *Kennels* Nantfforest, Llandovery, Carmarthenshire. *Meet* 6 days a fortnight.

TREDEGAR FARMERS'. *Country* Lies between Newport and Cardiff on the South and stretches 9 miles northwards from the Bristol Channel to the hills: *Kennels* Tredegar Park, Bassaleg, Mon. *Meet* Mon. and Thurs.

TYNEDALE. *Country* Northumberland: *Kennels* Stagshaw Bank, Corbridge-on-Tyne, Northumberland. *Meet* Mon., Wed., Sat.

TYNE, NORTH. *Country* N.W. Northumberland: *Kennels* Ealingham, Wark, Hexham, Northumberland. *Meet* Five days a fortnight.

ULLSWATER. *Country* Westmorland and Cumberland: *Kennels* Grassthwaite How, Glenridding, Cumberland. *Meet* Mon., Wed., Sat.

UNITED. *Country* Shropshire and Montgomeryshire: *Kennels* Bishops Castle, Shropshire. *Meet* Wed. and Sat.

VALE OF CLETTWR. *Country* North Carmarthenshire: *Kennels* Blaepant, Pencader, Carmarthenshire. *Meet* Tues. and Sat., occ. Thurs.

V.W.H. (EARL BATHURST'S). *Country*

Meet of the West Warwickshire Farmers' Hunt at Ye Olde King's Head.

Gloucestershire and Wiltshire: *Kennels* Cirencester Park, Glos. *Meet* Tues. and Sat.

V.W.H. (CRICKLADE). *Country* Gloucestershire, Wiltshire and Oxfordshire: *Kennels* Meyseyhampton, Fairford, Glos. *Meet* Tues., Thurs., Sat.

VINE. *Country* Hampshire with a small part in Berkshire: *Kennels* Hannington, Basingstoke, Hants. *Meet* Tues. and Sat.

WARWICKSHIRE. *Country* Warwickshire, Gloucestershire, Worcestershire and Oxfordshire: *Kennels* Kineton, Warwickshire. *Meet* Mon., Thurs., Sat.

WARWICKSHIRE FARMERS' (WEST). *Country* extends from Norton Lindsey westward to Worcestershire boundary and thence north to Brobey Vale: *Kennels* Temple Grafton Court, nr. Alcester. *Meet* Mon. and Thurs.

WARWICKSHIRE, NORTH. *Country* N. Warwickshire: *Kennels* Rouncil Lane, Kenilworth, Warwickshire. *Meet* Tues., Wed., Fri. and Sat.

WESTERN. *Country* W. Cornwall: *Kennels* Madron, Penzance, Cornwall. *Meet* Tues. and Fri.

WEST STREET. *Country* E. Kent: *Kennels* Solly Farm, Worth, nr. Deal, Kent. *Meet* Wed. and Sat.

WHADDON CHASE. *Country* Bucks.: *Kennels* Ascott, Wing, Bucks. *Meet* Tues. and Sat.

WHEATLAND. *Country* S. Shropshire: *Kennels* Eardington, Bridgnorth, Salop. *Meet* Wed. and Sat.

WILLIAMS-WYNN, SIR WATKIN. *Country* Denbigh, Flint, Cheshire and Shropshire: *Kennels* Wynnstay, Ruabon, Wrexham. *Meet* Mon. and Thurs.

WILTON. *Country* From south of Salisbury to the North Dorsetshire border: *Kennels* Wilton, nr. Salisbury, Hants. *Meet* Wed. and Sat.

WILTS., SOUTH AND WEST. *Country* between Wylye, Fovent, Shaftesbury, Gillingham, Shepton Mallet and Warminster: *Kennels* Motcombe, Shaftesbury, Dorset. *Meet* Mon., Wed., Sat.

WORCESTERSHIRE. *Country* Central part of Worcestershire: *Kennels* Farnhill Heath, nr. Worcester. *Meet* 5 days a fortnight.

WYLYE VALLEY. *Country* Extends to Bath and lies around Warminster, Westbury, Trowbridge and Salisbury Plain: *Kennels* Tytherington, Warminster, Wilts. *Meet* Wed. and Sat.

YNYSFOR. *Country* S. Caernarvonshire and N. Merioneth: *Kennels* Ynysfor, Penrhyndeudraeth, Merioneth. *Meet* Sat. A foot pack.

YORK AND AINSTY, NORTH. *Country* North and West Ridings of Yorkshire: *Kennels* Copgrove Hall, nr. Harrogate, Yorks. *Meet* Wed. and Sat.

YORK AND AINSTY, SOUTH. *Country* North, West and South of York: *Kennels* Acomb, York. *Meet* Tues. and Sat.

ZETLAND. *Country* S. Durham and N. Yorkshire: *Kennels* Aldborough St. John, Richmond, Yorks. *Meet* Tues., Thurs., Sat.

FOXHOUNDS—SCOTLAND

BERWICKSHIRE. *Country* Berwickshire: *Kennels* Briery Hills, Duns, Berwicks. *Meet* Tues. and Sat.

BUCCLEUCH'S, DUKE OF. *Country* Roxburghshire, Selkirk and Berwickshire: *Kennels* St. Boswells, Roxburghshire. *Meet* Mon., Wed., Thurs., Sat.

CHALLOCH. *Country* south west of Newton Stewart and east to Gatehouse of Ibort and Creetown: *Kennels* Challoch, Newton Stewart, Wigtownshire. *Meet* one day a week.

DUMFRIESSHIRE. *Country* Dumfriesshire: *Kennels* Glenholm, Lockerbie. *Meet* Tues. and Sat.

EGLINTON. *Country* Ayrshire: *Kennels* Earlston, Kilmarnock. *Meet* Wed., Sat., alt. Mon.

FIFE. *Country* Fifeshire: *Kennels* Harlswynd, Carrs, Fife. *Meet* Wed. and Sat.

JED FOREST *Country* Roxburghshire: *Kennels* Abotrule, Bouchester Bridge, Fife. *Meet* Wed. and Sat.

LANARKSHIRE AND RENFREWSHIRE. *Country* Renfrewshire. *Kennels* Houston, Renfrewshire. *Meet* Tues. and Sat.

LAUDERDALE. *Country* North of the railway from Greenlaw to Galashiels: *Kennels* Trabroun, Lauder, Berwickshire. *Meet* Tues. and Fri.

LIDDESDALE. *Country* Roxburghshire. *Kennels* Saughtree, Newcastleton. *Meet* 2 days a week.

LINLITHGOW AND STIRLINGSHIRE. *Country* Midlothian, West Lothian and Stirlingshire. *Kennels* Golfhall, Corstorphine, Edinburgh. *Meet* Sat., alt. Tues.

FOXHOUNDS—IRELAND

AVONDHU. *Country* Co. Cork: *Kennels* Corrinville, Fermoy. *Meet* Wed. and Sun.

BALLYMACAD. *Country* Co. Meath: *Kennels* Dromore, Oldcastle. *Meet* Tues., Fri. or Sat.

BERMINGHAM AND NORTH GALWAY. *Country* Cos. Galway and Mayo: *Kennels* Bermingham House, Tuam, Co. Galway. *Meet* alt. Sun. and Mon., Thurs.

BREE. *Country* Co. Wexford: *Kennels* Ballynadara, Enniscorthy, Co. Wexford. *Meet* Thurs. and Sat.

CARBERY. *Country* Co. Cork: *Kennels* Old Military Barracks, Bandon. *Meet* Thurs. and Sun.

CARLOW. *Country* Co. Carlow and Kildare: *Kennels* Moyle, Carlow. *Meet* Tues. and Sat.

DOWN, EAST. *Country* Round Downpatrick: *Kennels* Seaforde, Co. Down.

DUHALLOW. *Country* Northern part of Co. Cork: *Kennels* Blackrock, Mallow. *Meet* Mon., Wed., Fri., Sat.

COUNTY GALWAY (THE BLAZERS). *Country* Co. Galway: *Kennels* Craughwell, Co. Galway. *Meet* 3 days a week.

GOLDEN VALE. *Country* Co. Tipperary: *Kennels* Tullamaine, Fetlard. *Meet* Thurs. and bye.

ISLAND. *Country* Lies between Enniscorthy and Arklow, and Newtownburry and Kilmuckridge. *Kennels* Rockmount, Farns. *Meet* Tues., Thurs., Sat.

KILDARE. *Country* Cos. Kildare and West Wicklow with portions in Cos. Meath and Dublin. *Kennels* Jigginstown, Naas. *Meet* Tues., Thurs., Sat.

KILKENNY. *Country* Co. Kilkenny: *Kennels* Mount Juliet, Thomastown, Co. Kilkenny. *Meet* Mon., Wed., Sat.

KILKENNY, NORTH. *Country* N. of Co. Kilkenny: *Kennels* Ballyring, Freshford, Co. Kilkenny. *Meet* Fri.

LEIX (QUEEN'S COUNTY). *Country* Leix: *Kennels* Brechfield, Abbeybrix. *Meet* Wed. and Sat.

LIMERICK, Co. *Country* Co. Limerick:

Kennels Clonstire, Adare, Co. Limerick. *Meet* Mon., Wed., Fri.

LOUTH. *Country* Louth, Meath and Monaghan: *Kennels* Lissranny, Ardee, Co. Louth. *Meet* 2 days a week.

MEATH. *Country* Co. Meath. *Kennels* Nugentstown, Kells, Co. Meath. *Meet* Mon., Wed., Fri.

MUSKERRY. *Country* N. and S. of river Lee: *Kennels* Cloghroe, Blarney, Co. Cork. *Meet* Wed. and Sat.

ORMOND. *Country* from Longford Wood (East) to Lough Derg (West) and from Kimilty (North) to Cloughjordan (South). *Kennels* Knocknacree, Cloughjordan. Co. Tipperary. *Meet* Tues., alt. Sat.

SCARTEEN (BLACK AND TANS). *Country* Tipperary and Limerick: *Kennels* Scarteen, Knocklong: *Meet* Mon., Thurs. till end of Feb., then usually Tues. and Fri.

SHILLELAGH AND DISTRICT. *Country* Cos. Wicklow and Wexford (the old Coollattin country): *Kennels* Carnew Castle, Co. Wicklow. *Meet* Mon., Fri.

SOUTH UNION. *Country* Co. Cork: *Kennels* Furney, Carrigaline. *Meet* Tues. and Fri.

STRABANE. *Country* Borders of Cos. Tyrone and Donegal: *Kennels* Carricklee, Strabane, Co. Tyrone. *Meet* Wed. and Sat.

TIPPERARY. *Country* Co. Tipperary: *Kennels* Tullamaine, Fetlard, Co. Tipperary. *Meet* 4 days a week.

TIPPERARY, NORTH. *Country* North Riding of Co. Tipperary: *Kennels* Knocknacree, Cloughjordan, Co. Tipperary. *Meet* Thurs.

UNITED HUNT CLUB. *Country* Co. Cork: *Kennels* Knockgriffen, Midleton. *Meet* Tues., Fri.

WATERFORD. *Country* Between the sea (South) the River Suir (North) and the Comeragh mountains (West). *Kennels* Rockmount, Kilmacthomas, Co. Waterford. *Meet* Tues. and Sat.

WATERFORD, WEST. *Country* Bounded by U.H.C. in West, the Waterford in the East, and the Tipperary in the North. To the South is the sea: *Kennels* Bishopstown, Lismore. *Meet* Wed. and Sat. (Nov. to Jan.), thereafter Tues. and Sat.

WESTMEATH. *Country* Westmeath County: *Kennels* Cullene, Mullingar, Westmeath. *Meet* Mon., Wed., Fri.

WEXFORD. *Country* Co. Wexford: *Kennels* Moorfields, Ballinaboda, Wexford. *Meet* Tues. and Fri.

WICKLOW. *Country* S. Co. Wicklow and N. Co. Wexford: *Kennels* Knockbawn, Inch, Co. Wexford. *Meet* Wed. and Sat.

HARRIERS—
ENGLAND AND WALES

ALDENHAM. *Country* Herts., Bucks. and Beds. *Kennels* Puddephat's Farm, Markyate, Herts. *Meet* Wed. or Thurs., occ. Sat.

AXE VALE. *Country* S. E. Devon. *Kennels* Little Downhayne, Colyton, Devon. *Meet* Wed. and Sat.

BOLVENTOR. *Country* Cornwall: *Kennels* Norton, Bodmin. *Meet* Wed. (fox), Sat. (hare).

CAMBRIDGE FARMERS'. *Country* Around Cambridge: *Kennels* Old Tiles, Horningsea. *Meet* Tues. and Sat.

COTLEY. *Country* South of the Crewkerne-Honiton Road running north of the Honiton-Axminster railway to the sea at Charmouth. *Kennels* Cotley Wash, Membury, nr. Axminster. *Meet* Wed. and Sat.

CURY. *Country* The Lizard Peninsula:

Kennels Mawgan, nr. Helston. *Meet* Tues. and Sat.

DART VALE AND HALDON. *Country* S. Devon from Dart Valley to the Exe. *Kennels* Lonnard Mill, Week, Dartington, nr. Totnes. *Meet* Mon., Thurs., Sat.

DUNSTON. *Country* S. Norfolk: *Kennels* Kenningham Hall, Mulbarton, Norwich. *Meet* Tues. and Fri.

EASTON. *Country* E. Suffolk: *Kennels* Easton, Woodbridge, Suffolk. *Meet* Mon. and Thurs.

HIGH PEAK. *Country* Around Bakewell and Buxton in Derbyshire: *Kennels* The Shutts, Bakewell, Derbyshire. *Meet* Wed. and Sat.

HOLCOMBE. *Country* Lancashire, west of Rossendale and south of the Ribble. *Kennels* Kirklees, Brandlesholme, nr. Bury. *Meet* Wed. and Sat.

MINEHEAD. *Country* W. Somerset: *Kennels* Huntsham, Wootton Courtenay, Minehead, Som. *Meet* Wed. and Sat.

MODBURY. *Country* S. Devon: *Kennels* Modbury, Devon. *Meet* Tues., Fri. or Sat.

MONTGOMERY. *Country* The Clun Forest: *Kennels* Anchor Inn, Newcastle, Salop. *Meet* Tues. and Sat. (A private pack, formerly the Brecon Harriers.)

NORFOLK, NORTH. *Country* Lies north of a line from Bandeswell on the west side to Ludham on the east, to the coast. *Kennels* Melton Constable Park, Norfolk. *Meet* Mon. and Thurs.

PENDLE FOREST AND CRAVEN. *Country* East Lancs. and West Riding of Yorks.: *Kennels* Ellenthorpe, Gisburn via Clitheroe. *Meet* Tues., Sat., occ. Thurs.

ROCKWOOD. *Country* West Riding of Yorks.: *Kennels* Meal Hill, New Mill, nr. Huddersfield. *Meet* Wed. and Sat.

ROSS. *Country* S. Hereford: *Kennels* New House, Goodrich, Ross-on-Wye. *Meet* Tues. and Fri.

SENNOWE PARK. *Country* A private estate in Norfolk. *Kennels* Sennowe Park, Guist, Norfolk. *Meet* Usually Tues. and Sat. A private pack.

SINCLAIR'S, MR. *Country* That previously hunted by the Wensleydale Harriers between Aysgarth and Hawes: *Kennels* Southwoods Hall, Thirsk, Yorks.: *Meet* 2 days a week.

SOUTH POOL. *Country* S. Devon: *Kennels* Chillington, Devon. *Meet* Tues. and Sat.

SPARKFORD VALE. *Country* S. E. Somerset: *Kennels* Wales, Quarn Camel, nr. Yeovil. *Meet* Wed. and Sat.

TAUNTON VALE. *Country* Somerset: *Kennels* Blackbrook, Som. *Meet* Mon., Thurs., occ. Sat.

VALE OF LUNE. *Country* On the borders of Lancashire, Westmorland and Yorkshire: *Kennels* Hornby, nr. Lancaster. *Meet* Wed. and Sat.

WAVENEY VALLEY. *Country* In Norfolk and Suffolk: *Kennels* Grove Farm, Raveningham, Norfolk. *Meet* Tues. and Sat.

WESTON. *Country* Somerset: *Kennels* Webbington, Axbridge, Som. *Meet* Wed. and Sat.

WINDERMERE. *Country* Lake District: *Kennels* Dungeon Ghyll, Langdale, Westmorland. *Meet* 3 days a week.

HARRIERS—IRELAND

ANTRIM, EAST. *Country* Between Belfast, Antrim and Larne: *Kennels* Ballysavage, Templepatrick, Co. Antrim. *Meet* Wed. and Sat.

ANTRIM, MID. *Country* Mid Antrim: *Kennels* Galgorm Park, Ballymena. *Meet* Tues. and Sat.

BRAY. *Country* Cos. Wicklow and

Dublin: *Kennels* Lehamstown Park, Cabinterly, Co. Dublin. *Meet* Tues., Sat.

CLARE, Co. *Country* Adjacent to Shannon Airport: *Kennels* Ballycar, Newmarket-on-Fargus, Co. Clare. *Meet* Mon., Thurs.

CLONMEL. *Country* Southern part of Tipperary Foxhounds Country: *Kennels* Heywood Road, Clonmel. *Meet* Tues. and Fri.

CROOM. *Country* Mid and East Limerick: *Kennels* Liskennett House, Croom, Co. Limerick. *Meet* Tues. and occ. bye.

DERRY, SOUTH. *Country* West of that of the Mid-Antrim and S.E. of the Strabane Foxhounds: *Kennels* White Hill, Bellaghy, Co. Derry. *Meet* Wed. and Sat.

DOWN, NORTH. *Country* Northern part of Co. Down: *Kennels* Islandhill Road, Camber, Co. Down. *Meet* Wed. and Sat.

DUBLIN, CO., SOUTH. *Country* Around Rathcoola, Blackchurch and Tallaght: *Kennels* Dundrum, Co. Dublin. *Meet* Wed. and Sat.

DUNGARVAN. *Country* From east of Cappoquin to Youghal Bridge and as far as Clonea Castle and the Pike.

Kennels Youghal Road, Dungarvan, Co. Waterford. *Meet* Sun. and byes.

FERMANAGH. *Country* All Co. Fermanagh and adjoining parts of Co. Monaghan, Co. Tyrone and Co. Donegal: *Kennels* Castlecool, Enniskillen, Co. Fermanagh. *Meet* Wed. and Sat.

FINGAL. *Country* N. Co. Dublin and S. Co. Meath: *Kennels* Coolquay, The Ward, Co. Dublin. *Meet* Tues. and Fri.

IVEAGH. *Country* Co. Down and North Armagh: *Kennels* Tonnaghmore, Banbridge. *Meet* Wed. and Sat.

KILDARE, NORTH. *Country* N. Kildare and S. Meath: *Kennels* Laragh House, Maynooth, Co. Kildare. *Meet* Mon. and Thurs.

KILLINICK. *Country* S. E. corner of Co. Wexford: *Kennels* Thornville, Co. Wexford. *Meet* Mon. and Thurs.

KILLULTAGH, OLDROCK AND CHICHESTER. *Country* From Ballinderry to Antrim, South of Lough Neagh: *Kennels* Dundrod, Co. Antrim. *Meet* Wed. and Sat.

KILMOGANNY. *Country* Around Castlejohn and Kilmoganny: *Kennels* Castletown House, Carrick-on-Suir, Co. Kilkenny. *Meet* 2 days a week.

LIMERICK. *Country* Co. Limerick: *Kennels* Derryknockane, Limerick. *Meet* Thurs., occ. bye.

LITTLEGRANGE. *Country* E. Co. Meath and S. Co. Louth: *Kennels* Lisdornan, Julianstown, Co. Meath. *Meet* Mon. and Thurs.

LONGFORD, CO. *Country* Around Longford, Granard, Ballymahon and Edgeworthstown: *Kennels* Balliuree, Edgeworthstown, Co. Longford. *Meet* Tues. and Fri.

MAYO, NORTH. *Country* N. Mayo and W. Sligo: *Kennels* Barnfield House, Ballina, Co. Mayo. *Meet* Thurs. and byes.

MONKSTOWN. *Country* Around Cork City: *Kennels* Glen Road, Monkstown. *Meet* Sun., occ. bye.

NAAS. *Country* Around Naas, Kilcullen, Kildare and Clare: *Kennels* New Abbey, Kilcullen, Co. Kildare. *Meet* Wed. and Fri.

NEWRY. *Country* S. Co. Down and Co. Armagh: *Kennels* Drumbanagher, Jerrettspass, Newry, Co. Down. *Meet* Tues. and Sat.

RAKES OF MALLOW. *Country* Around

Mallow and Annakisha: *Kennels* Mallow, Co. Cork. *Meet* Sun. and byes.

ROUTE. *Country* N. Co. Londonderry: *Kennels* Crossreagh, Portrush. *Meet* Wed. and Sat.

SLIGO, Co. *Country* Sligo: *Kennels* Cleverhill House, Sligo. *Meet* Wed. and byes.

SLIGO, Co. (SOUTH). *Country* S.W. part of Co. Sligo: *Kennels* Bollinlig House, Beltra, Co. Sligo. *Meet* Tues. and Fri.

TARA. *Country* Co. Meath: *Kennels* Bective House, Navan, Co. Meath. *Meet* Mon. and Thurs.

TYNAN AND ARMAGH. *Country* In Armagh and Tyrone: *Meet* Wed. and Sat. A trencher-fed pack.

STAGHOUNDS—ENGLAND

DEVON AND SOMERSET. *Country* W. Somerset and N. Devon: *Kennels* Exford. *Meet* Tues., Thurs., Sat.

KENT, MID. *Country* Mid and East Kent: *Kennels* Bicknor Farm, Langley, Kent. *Meet* Wed. and Sat.

NEW FOREST BUCKHOUNDS. *Country* New Forest: *Kennels* Brockenhurst. *Meet* Mon. and Fri.

NORWICH. *Country* S. Norfolk: *Kennels* Wacton House, Norwich. *Meet* Mon. and Thurs.

QUANTOCK. *Country* The Quantock Hills: *Kennels* Bagborough. *Meet* Mon. and Thurs.

SAVERNAKE FOREST BUCKHOUNDS. *Country* Around Marlborough and Hungerford. *Kennels* Savernake Home Farm, nr. Marlborough, Wilts. *Meet* Wed.

TIVERTON. *Country* Devon: *Kennels* Leigh Barton, Loxbeare, Tiverton. *Meet* Sat. and one other day per fortnight.

STAGHOUNDS—IRELAND

DOWN, COUNTY. *Country* Co. Down: *Kennels* Rockmount, Ballykine, Ballynahinch, Co. Down. *Meet* Tues. and Sat.

WARD UNION. *Country* N. Co. Dublin and S. Co. Meath: *Kennels* Ashbourne, Co. Meath. *Meet* Tues. and Sat.

DRAGHOUNDS—GREAT BRITAIN

CAMBRIDGE UNIVERSITY. *Country* Around Cambridge: *Kennels* Barton Road, Cambridge. *Meet* every Mon. of Term; bye Thurs. A private pack.

MID-SURREY FARMERS'. *Country* In the Old Surrey and Burstow, West Kent;

Southdown and Surrey Union by permission of the Masters: *Kennels* Newchapel, Lingfield, Surrey. *Meet* Sat.

NORTH EAST CHESHIRE. *Country* Bounded in the North by the Mossley-Holmefirth Road and in the South by the Macclesfield-Chapel-en-le-Frith Road. *Kennels* Woodseats Lane, Charlesworth. *Meet* Sat.

OXFORD UNIVERSITY. *Country* Around Oxford and Bicester by permission of the Bicester and Heythrop Hunts: *Kennels* Garsington, Oxford. *Meet* Wed. or Fri.

ROYAL ENGINEERS. *Country* By permission of the Tickham and West Kent Hunts. *Kennels* Brompton Barracks, Chatham. *Meet* Tues. or Wed., Sat.

STAFF COLLEGE. *Country* Around Wokingham, Eversley and Holyport by permission of the Garth Hunt: *Kennels* Staff College, Camberley, Surrey. *Meet* Wed.

FOOT HARRIERS AND BEAGLES— ENGLAND AND WALES

AIREDALE BEAGLES. *Country* In Airedale and Wharfedale: *Kennels* Eldwick, nr. Bingley, Yorks. *Meet* Wed. and Sat.

ALDERSHOT BEAGLES. *Country* Aldershot-Farnham-Allou Area. *Kennels* Oxney Farm, Bordon. *Meet* Wed. and Sat.

AMPLEFORTH COLLEGE BEAGLES. *Country* Around Ampleforth, Helmsley, Kirby Moorside and Pickering: *Kennels* Gilling Castle, Gilling East, Yorks. *Meet* Wed. and Sat.

ANGLESEY BEAGLES. *Country* Anglesey: *Kennels* Llangefin, Anglesey. *Meet* Tues. and Sat.

BEACON BEAGLES. *Country* Somerset and N.E. Devon: *Kennels* Holcombe, Hemyock. *Meet* Wed., Sat.

BERKELEY, OLD, BEAGLES. *Country* Bucks., Herts. and Oxon. *Kennels* Beamond End, nr. Amersham, Bucks. *Meet* Wed. and Sat.

BLACK COMBE BEAGLES. *Country* W. Cumberland: *Kennels* Bootle. *Meet* 5 days a fortnight.

BLEAN BEAGLES. *Country* Kent: *Kennels* Waterham Farm, Hernhill, Faversham, Kent. *Meet* Wed. and Sat.

BLEASDALE BEAGLES. *Country* N. Lancs., S. Westmorland and West Riding of Yorks.: *Kennels* Killington, nr. Sedbergh, Yorks. *Meet* Tues. and Sat.

BOLEBROKE BEAGLES. *Country* West

Kent: *Kennels* Crowdleham. *Meet* Wed. and Sat.

BRIGHTON AND STORRINGTON FOOT BEAGLES. *Country* Sussex: *Kennels* Clappers Lane, Fulking, Poynings, Sussex. *Meet* Sat., alt. Wed.

BRITANNIA BEAGLES. *Country* Around Dartmouth: *Kennels* Britannia Royal Naval College, Dartmouth. *Meet* Wed. and Sat.

BUCKS., NORTH, BEAGLES. *Country* N. Bucks. and W. Beds.: *Kennels* Putnor Farm, Bedford. *Meet* Thurs. and Sat.

CASTLETON BEAGLES. *Country* Between Newport and Cardiff. *Kennels* Red Barn, Castleton, nr. Cardiff. *Meet* Sat. and bye.

CATTERICK BEAGLES. *Country* Around Catterick, Richmond and Leyburn. *Kennels* White House Farm, Waitwith, Catterick Camp, Yorks. *Meet* Wed. and Sat.

CHESHIRE BEAGLES. *Country* Around Chester: *Kennels* Dodleston, Cheshire. *Meet* Wed. and Sat.

CHILMARK BEAGLES. *Country* Wilts., Hants. and Dorset: *Kennels* Chilmark, nr. Salisbury. *Meet* Mon., Sat.

CHRIST CHURCH AND NEW COLLEGE BEAGLES. *Country* N., E. and W. of Oxford. *Kennels* Garsington, Oxon. *Meet* Mon., Wed., Sat.

CLARO BEAGLES. *Country* Around Harrogate, Ripon and Wetherby: *Kennels* Field House Farm, Darley, Harrogate. *Meet* Tues. and Sat.

CLIFTON FOOT HARRIERS. *Country* N. Somerset: *Kennels* Yalton, Som. *Meet* Sat. and frequent Weds.

COLCHESTER GARRISON BEAGLES. *Country* A 15-mile radius of Colchester: *Kennels* Berechurch Camp, Colchester. *Meet* Wed. and Sat. (occ. Tues., Thurs., Sat.).

COLNE VALLEY. *Country* Around Huddersfield and Halifax: *Kennels* Butternab Wood, Beaumont Park, Huddersfield, Yorks. *Meet* Sat., occ. Wed.

DALGETY'S, MR. *Country* The Hursley Foxhound Country: *Kennels* Hursley Hunt Kennels, Braishfield, Hants. *Meet* one day a week and bye. A private pack.

DARTMOOR, NORTH, BEAGLES. *Country* Around Chagford: *Kennels* Chagford, Devon. *Meet* Wed. or Thurs. A private pack.

DERWENT VALLEY BEAGLES. *Country* In the Middleton and York and Ainsty country: *Kennels* Westow Lodge, Whitwell-on-the-Hill. *Meet* Sat. and occ. byes.

DUMMER BEAGLES. *Country* North Cotswolds: *Kennels* Little Rissington Manor, nr. Cheltenham, Glos. *Meet* Tues. and Sat.

ECCLESFIELD BEAGLES. *Country* West Riding of Yorks.: *Kennels* Townsend Road, Ecclesfield, nr. Sheffield. *Meet* Thurs. and Sat.

ENGLISH'S, MRS., BEAGLES. *Country* Norfolk around King's Lynn: *Kennels* Bridge House, Gayton, King's Lynn. *Meet* Sat. A private pack.

ESSEX, MID, BEAGLES. *Country* Around Chelmsford: *Kennels* Spurriers, Norton Heath, nr. Ingatestone, Essex. *Meet* Wed., Sat., occ. bye Mon.

ESSEX, NORTH, FOOT BEAGLES. *Country* N. E. Essex: *Kennels* Mullets Farm, Stock, Essex. *Meet* Tues. (twice monthly) and Sat.

ETON COLLEGE BEAGLES. *Country* Around Eton and Windsor. *Kennels* Eton College, Windsor. *Meet* Tues., Thurs., Sat. (Tues. and Sat. only until Dec. 1st.)

FARLEY HILL BEAGLES. *Country* Around Wokingham and Basingstoke: *Kennels* Bensgrove Farm, Goring Heath, Oxon. *Meet* Wed. and Sat.

FOREST AND DISTRICT BEAGLES. *Country* E. Cheshire: *Kennels* Long Ridge, Sutton, Macclesfield, Cheshire. *Meet* Sat.

GARRON VALLEY BEAGLES. *Country* Herefordshire: *Kennels* Rhydicar Farm, St. Weonards, Hereford. *Meet* Sat.

GEACH'S, MR. HARRY, BEAGLES. *Country* Around Retford, Gainsborough and Market Rasen: *Kennels* Mill House, Walesby, nr. Market Rasen, Lincs. *Meet* Sat.

GLYN CELYN BEAGLES (formerly Caldbeck Fell Beagles). *Country* Around Builth Wells: *Kennels* Verlands, Crickadaru, Erwood, nr. Builth Wells. *Meet* variable. A private pack.

HERTS., SOUTH, BEAGLES. *Country* Herts. and Beds. *Kennels* Church Lodge, Stagenhoe, Whitwell, Herts. *Meet* Sat., occ. bye.

HOLME VALLEY BEAGLES. *Country* West Riding of Yorkshire: *Kennels* Upperthong, nr. Holmfirth, Yorks. *Meet* Sat.

ILMINSTER BEAGLES. *Country* Around Ilminster, Som. *Kennels* Trencher-fed. *Meet* Sat., alt. Thurs.

173

ISLE OF WIGHT FOOT BEAGLES. *Country* Isle of Wight: *Kennels* Gatacombe, Newport, I.O.W. *Meet* Sat., occ. bye.

MARLBOROUGH COLLEGE BEAGLES. *Country* Wilts. *Kennels* Marlborough College, Wilts. *Meet* Tues. and Sat.

MEON VALLEY AND WINCHESTER BEAGLES. *Country* Around Bishop's Waltham and Winchester: *Kennels* West End House, Hambledon. *Meet* Tues. and Sat.

NEWCASTLE AND DISTRICT BEAGLES. *Country* S. Northumberland: *Kennels* High Street, Heddon-on-the-Wall, Northumberland. *Meet* Sat., occ. bye.

NEW FOREST BEAGLES. *Country* New Forest: *Kennels* Bartley, Southampton. *Meet* Sat.

PER ARDUA (R.A.F.) BEAGLES. *Country* Lincs. and Notts.: *Kennels* R.A.F. College, Cranwell, Sleaford, Lincs. *Meet* Wed., Sat., occ. Thurs.

PEVENSEY MARSH BEAGLES. *Country* Around Pevensey and the Rother Valley: *Kennels* Highwoods Farm, Wydown, Bexhill-on-Sea. *Meet* Wed. and Sat.

PIMPERNEL BEAGLES. *Country* N. and E. Dorset: *Kennels* Blandford Camp, Dorset. *Meet* Wed. and Sat.

PIPEWELL FOOT BEAGLES. *Country* Northants: *Kennels* Pipewell, near Kettering. *Meet* Thurs. and Sat.

RADLEY COLLEGE BEAGLES. *Country* Around Abingdon, Didcot and Radley: *Kennels* Radley College, nr. Abingdon. *Meet* Tues., Sat., occ. Thurs.

ROCHDALE AND PENNINE FOOT HARRIERS. *Country* Around Rochdale. *Kennels* Sparth, Rochdale, Lancs. *Meet* Sat., occ. Tues.

ROYAL AGRICULTURAL COLLEGE BEAGLES. *Country* Around Cirencester. *Kennels* Coates, nr. Cirencester. *Meet* Wed. and Sat.

ROYAL ROCK BEAGLES. *Country* Between Chester and Birkenhead: *Kennels* Ledsham, nr. Chester. *Meet* Sat., alt. Wed.

SANDHURST BEAGLES. *Country* Around Camberley and Basingstoke: *Kennels* R.M.A. Sandhurst, Camberley, Surrey. *Meet* Wed., bye, Sat.

SCHOOL OF INFANTRY BEAGLES. *Country* Wilts. and Somerset: *Kennels* School of Infantry, Warminster. *Meet* Wed. and Sat.

SHROPSHIRE BEAGLES. *Country* Around Shrewsbury and Wellington. *Kennels*

Grove House, Rodington, Shrewsbury. *Meet* Tues., Wed. or Sat.

SPROUGHTON FOOT BEAGLES. *Country* S.E. Suffolk: *Kennels* Pigeon Lane, Washbrook, Ipswich. *Meet* Sat., occ. Wed.

STAFFORDSHIRE BEAGLES. *Country* S. Staffs. and parts of Shropshire and Warwickshire: *Kennels* Newton, nr. Walsall, Staffs. *Meet* Wed. and Sat.

STAFFORDSHIRE, NORTH, MOORLAND BEAGLES. *Country* N. Staffs.: *Kennels* Heenheath Farm, Trentham, Staffs. *Meet* Sat., occ. bye.

STEWARD'S, MR., BEAGLES. *Country* Notts. south of the Trent and N. Leicestershire: *Kennels* St. James's Street, Nottingham. *Meet* Wed., occ. Sat.

STOKE HILL BEAGLES. *Country* Around Exeter, Exmouth and Tiverton: *Kennels* Trumps, Aylesbeare, E. Devon. *Meet* Tues. or Wed., Sat.

STOKESLEY FARMERS' BEAGLES. *Country* N. Yorks. and S. Durham. *Kennels* Greenhow Moor, Nunthorpe, Middlesbrough. *Meet* Sat.

SURREY, WEST, AND HORSELL BEAGLES. *Country* East to West Dorking to Chobham, North to South Chessington to the North Downs and South to Horsham: *Kennels* Dog Kennel Green, Ranmore, Dorking. *Meet* Wed. and Sat.

TEES VALLEY BEAGLES. *Country* Tees Valley: *Kennels* Streatham Camp, Barnard Castle. *Meet* Wed. and Sat.

TIR LARL BEAGLES. *Country* Glamorgan: *Kennels* Garn Wen Road, Nantyffyllon. *Meet* Sat.

TRINITY FOOT BEAGLES. *Country* N. and W. of Cambridge: *Kennels* Barton, Cambs. *Meet* Tues., Thurs., Sat.

VALE OF CLWYD. *Country* Vale of Clwyd: *Kennels* Erw Vran, Denbigh. *Meet* Sat., occ. bye.

WARWICKSHIRE BEAGLES. *Country* Warwickshire, Worcestershire and parts of North Cotswolds: *Kennels* Brobey, nr. Redditch. *Meet* Wed. and Sat.

WEARDALE BEAGLES. *Country* Around Stanhope, Lanchester and Durham: *Kennels* The Dene, Stanhope, Co. Durham. *Meet* Wed. and Sat.

WICK AND DISTRICT BEAGLES. *Country* Sodbury Vale, Gloucestershire and Somerset: *Kennels* Old Rectory, Syston, Mangotsfield, nr. Bristol. *Meet* Wed. and Sat.

WORCESTER PARK AND BUCKLAND

BEAGLES. *Country* Around Reigate, Oxted, Horley, Lingfield, East Grinstead: *Kennels* Mugswell, Chipstead. *Meet* Sat., alt. Tues.

WYE COLLEGE BEAGLES. *Country* Around Wye and Ashford: *Kennels* Coldharbour, Wye. *Meet* Tues. or Wed., Sat.

WYRE FOREST BEAGLES. *Country* N. and W. Worcs., S. Shropshire and parts of Herefordshire, Radnorshire and Montgomeryshire: *Kennels* Moat Farm, Tibberton, nr. Droitwich, Worcester. *Meet* Sat., occ. Thurs.

FOOT HARRIERS AND BEAGLES— SCOTLAND

CASTLE MILK FOOT HARRIERS. *Country* Dumfriesshire: *Kennels* Castle Milk, Lockerbie, Dumfriesshire. *Meet* Mon. and Fri. A private pack.

ETTRICK-FOREST BEAGLES. *Country* Selkirkshire and parts of Roxburghshire: *Kennels* Rutherford, Kelso, Roxburghshire (bitches); Hyndhope, Ettrick, Selkirkshire (dog hounds). *Meet* Tues. and Fri. A private pack.

FOOT HARRIERS AND BEAGLES— IRELAND

ARMAGH AND DISTRICT BEAGLES. *Country* A 3-mile radius of Armagh City. *Kennels* Trencher-fed. *Meet* Wed. and Sat.

CASHEL BEAGLES. *Country* Golden Valley of Co. Tipperary: *Meet* Sun.

CORDUFF BEAGLES. *Country* N. E. Co. Dublin: *Kennels* Corduff House, Lusk, Co. Dublin. *Meet* alt. Sat. and Sun., bye Thurs.

CURRAGH FOOT BEAGLES. *Country* Co. Kildare: *Kennels* Curragh Camp. *Meet* Sun. and Wed.

GOLDBURN BEAGLES. *Country* S. Co. Dublin and Co. Meath: *Kennels* Main Street, Danboyne. *Meet* Sun. and Wed.

GOREY AND DISTRICT BEAGLES. *Country* N. Co. Wexford and S. Co. Wicklow: *Kennels* Raheenagurrin, Gorey, Co. Wexford. *Meet* Sun.

HOLYCROSS BEAGLES. *Country* Central Tipperary: *Kennels* Inch, Thurlee, Co. Tipperary. *Meet* Sun. and Wed.

KILFEACLE BEAGLES. *Country* Golden Vale (Tipperary-Limerick borders): *Kennels* Kennelled during hunting Season; trencher-fed in off season. *Meet* Sun. and byes.

MARYBOROUGH FOOT BEAGLES. *Country* S.E. of Cork City: *Kennels* Laplands, Douglas, Co. Cork. *Meet* Sun.

MIDLETON FOOT BEAGLES. *Country* S.E. portion of Co. Cork: *Kennels* Avoncore, Midleton, Co. Cork. *Meet* Sun. and byes.

RIVERSTOWN BEAGLES. *Country* Riverstown, 5 miles from Cork City: *Kennels* Riverstown, Co. Cork. *Meet* Sun.

WATERVILLE BEAGLES. *Country* Waterville, Co. Kerry: *Kennels* Hounds kept by Members of the Beagle Club. *Meet* Sun., Wed.

WELFORT BEAGLES. *Country* Around Tullamore and Ballinasloe: *Kennels* Rahan Lodge, Tullamore, Co. Offaly. *Meet* Sun., Wed.

BASSET HOUNDS— GREAT BRITAIN

CRAIGCLEUCH. *Country* S.W. Dumfriesshire and in the neighbourhood of York: *Kennels* Craigcleugh, Langholm, Dumfriesshire. *Meet* Wed. or Sat. A private pack.

CROWCOMBE. *Country* W. Somerset: *Kennels* Crowcombe Court, Taunton: *Meet* One day a week. A private pack.

DE BURGH. *Country* Cambridgeshire and Suffolk borders: *Kennels* Brettons, Burrough Green, Newmarket. *Meet* Wed. and Sat.

GRIMS. *Country* Around Andover, Newbury and Whitechurch: *Kennels* Rooks Nest, Tuppen, nr. Newbury, Berks. *Meet* Wed., occ. bye.

HEREFORDSHIRE. *Country* Northern half of Herefordshire: *Kennels* The Firs, Kilpeck, Herefordshire. *Meet* Sat., occ. bye.

WARWICKSHIRE, NORTH, HAREHOUNDS. *Country* N. Warwickshire and W. Leicestershire: *Kennels* Grammar School Farm, Coleshill, Warwickshire. *Meet* Sat. and occ. bye.

WESTERBY. *Country* Around Market Harborough and Lutterworth: *Kennels* The Grange, Saddington, Leics. *Meet* Tues. and Sat.

WEST LODGE HAREHOUNDS. *Country* Around Elstree, Radlett, St. Albans, Hatfield, Hertford and Nazeing: *Kennels* Oaklands Lane, Arkley, Barnet. *Meet* Sat. and occ. bye.

CHAPTER FIFTEEN

Regulations governing
Point-to-Point Steeplechases

With the sanction of the Stewards of the National Hunt Committee, Point-to-Point Steeplechases may be held on one day annually by:—

(a) A Hunt, or two or more adjoining Hunts, being Foxhounds, Staghounds, Harriers (the Master being a Member of the Association of Masters of Harriers), or Military Draghounds.

In the case of Staghounds, Harriers or Military Draghounds, if the races are to be held in a country hunted by Foxhounds, the written permission of the Master of such Foxhounds must accompany the application.

(b) By the Royal Navy, the Army, the Royal Air Force, or by the United Services, or by a Naval or Military Formation or Unit or by a Club or other Society approved by the Stewards of the National Hunt Committee.

The written permission of the Master of Foxhounds, or, if in a district not hunted by Foxhounds, the Master of Staghounds or Harriers (being a Member of the Association of Masters of Harriers) hunting the same, in whose country it is proposed to run, must accompany the application in these cases.

Hunt Point-to-Point Steeplechases shall be held under the control of the Master of Hounds and of a Committee appointed by him.

Point-to-Points are usually held during the period from the beginning of February to the beginning of May.

The Course must be not less than 3 miles in length and all the horses competing must have been fairly hunted during the Season holding a Master of Hounds' Certificate to that effect. Every meeting must have at least one Race confined to members of the Hunt or other "unit" authorised to hold the meeting.

Not more than one race may be an "Open" Race for which horses from any hunt may compete. The other races must be confined to Members of or Farmers in the Hunt sponsoring the Meeting or Hunts adjacent to the sponsoring Hunt.

The number of Races is limited to 5 unless a special race such as a Regimental Race is included, in which case 6 races are permitted. Ladies may only ride in a race confined to Lady Riders and only one of these may be included at any meeting.

CHAPTER SIXTEEN

List of Point-to-Point Steeplechases

ALBRIGHTON at Wilbrighton (*Salop*).
ALBRIGHTON WOODLAND at Chaddesley Corbett (*Salop*).
ALDENHAM HARRIERS at Friars Wash (*Herts.*).
ARMY at Tweseldown (*Hants.*).
ASHFORD VALLEY at Charing (*Kent*).
ATHERSTONE at Clifton-upon-Dunsmore (*Warwicks.*).
AVON VALE at Monkton Farleigh (*Wilts.*).
AXE VALE HARRIERS at Stafford Cross (*Devon*).
AYRSHIRE YEOMANRY at Tarbolton (*Scotland*).
BADSWORTH at Bretton (*Yorks.*).
THE DUKE OF BEAUFORT'S at Didmarton (*Glos.*).
BEDALE at Bedale (*Yorks.*).
BELVOIR at Garthorpe (*Leics.*).
BERKELEY at Woodford (*Glos.*).
OLD BERKELEY at Kimble (*Bucks.*).

OLD BERKSHIRE at Lockinge (*Berks.*).
SOUTH BERKSHIRE at Tweseldown (*Hants.*).
BICESTER AND WARDEN HILL at Kimble (*Bucks.*).
BLACKMORE VALE at Oborne (*Dorset*).
BLANKNEY at Boothby Graffoe (*Lincs.*).
BOLVENTOR HARRIERS at Lemalia (*Cornwall*).
BORDER HUNTS at Drakemyre (*Scotland*).
BRAES OF DERWENT at Whittonstall (*Northumberland*).
BRAMHAM MOOR at Swindon Moor (*Yorks.*).
BROCKLESBY at Brocklesby (*Lincs.*).
DUKE OF BUCCLEUCH'S AND JEDFOREST at Friars Laugh (*Scotland*).
BURTON at Burton (*Lincs.*).
CAMBRIDGESHIRE at Hanningford Abbots (*Cambs.*).
CAMBRIDGE UNIVERSITY at Marks Tey (*Essex*).

CAMBRIDGE UNIVERSITY UNITED HUNTS CLUB at Cottenham (*Cambs.*).
CATTISTOCK at East Coker (*Dorset*).
CHESHIRE at Alpraham (*Cheshire*).
CHESHIRE FOREST at Littleton (*Cheshire*).

CHIDDINGFOLD AND LECONFIELD at Tismans (*Surrey*).
CHIDDINGFOLD FARMERS' at Peper Harrow (*Surrey*).
CLEVELAND at Little Ayton (*Yorks.*).

The Ladies' race, Aldenham Harriers Point-to-Point.

CLIFTON-ON-TEME at Horsham (*Worcs.*).
EAST CORNWALL at Lemalia (*Cornwall*).
NORTH CORNWALL at Bodmin (*Cornwall*).
COTLEY AND SEAVINGTON at Cotley (*Som.*).
COTSWOLD at Andoversford (*Glos.*).
NORTH COTSWOLD at Springhill (*Glos.*).
COTSWOLD VALE FARMERS' at Bushley Park (*Glos.*).
COTTESMORE at Whissendine (*Rutland*).
COWDRAY at Midhurst (*Sussex*).
CRAVEN FARMERS' at Lockinge (*Berks.*).
CRAWLEY AND HORSHAM at Storrington (*Sussex*).
CROOME at Upton-on-Severn (*Worcs.*).
CUMBERLAND at Bewaldeth (*Cumberland*).
CUMBERLAND FARMERS' at Dalston (*Cumberland*).
CURRE at Howick (*Mon.*).
CURY HARRIERS at Tehiay (*Cornwall*).
DARTMOOR at Stippadon (*Devon*).
DART VALE AND HALDON HARRIERS at Totnes (*Devon*).
DERWENT at Wykeham (*Yorks.*).
DEVON AND SOMERSET STAGHOUNDS at Holmcote (*Devon*).
EAST DEVON at Clyst St. Mary (*Devon*).

MID-DEVON at Moretonhampstead (*Devon*).
SOUTH DEVON at Forcher Cross (*Devon*).
SOUTH DORSET at Wareham (*Dorset*).
EAST DULVERTON at Venford (*Devon*).
WEST DULVERTON at Bratton Down (*Devon*).
DUMFRIESSHIRE at Roberthill (*Scotland*).
DUNSTON HARRIERS at Hethersett (*Norfk.*)
SOUTH DURHAM at Sedgefield (*Durham*).
EASTON HARRIERS at Hasketon (*Suffolk*).
EGGESFORD at Loosebeare (*Devon*).
EGLINTON at Tarbolton (*Scotland*).
ENFIELD CHACE at Enfield (*Herts.*).
ERIDGE at Kippings Cross (*Kent*).
ESSEX at Hatfield Broad Oak (*Essex*).
ESSEX AND SUFFOLK at Higham (*Essex*).
EAST ESSEX at Marks Tey (*Essex*).
ESSEX FARMERS' at Beeleigh (*Essex*).
ESSEX UNION at Hatfield Broad Oak (*Essex*).
EXMOOR at Bratton Down (*Devon*).
FERNIE at Dingley (*Leics.*).
FIFE at Balcormo (*Scotland*).
FITZWILLIAM at Waternewton (*Northants.*).
FLINT AND DENBIGH at Criccin (*Flint*).
FOUR BURROW at Tehidy (*Cornwall*).
GARTH at Tweseldown (*Hants.*).

GLAMORGAN at Penllyn (*Glam.*).

GOLDEN VALLEY at Bredwardine (*Hereford*).

GRAFTON at Pattishall (*Northants.*).

GROVE AND RUFFORD at Markham Moor (*Notts.*).

HAMBLEDON at Pitt Manor (*Hants.*).

HAMPSHIRE at Hackwood Park (*Hants.*).

HARKAWAY CLUB at Chaddesley Corbett (*Salop*).

HAYDON at Lunestone Bank (*Northumberland*).

NORTH HEREFORDSHIRE at Newtown (*Hereford*).

SOUTH HEREFORDSHIRE at Belmont (*Hereford*).

HERTFORDSHIRE at Friars Wash (*Herts.*).

HEYTHROP at Stow-on-the-Wold (*Glos.*).

HIGH PEAK HARRIERS at Flagg Moor (*Derby*).

HOLCOMBE HARRIERS at Nab Gate (*Lancs.*).

HOLDERNESS at Dalton Park (*Yorks.*).

HOUSEHOLD BRIGADE AND CAVALRY CLUB at Crowell (*Oxon.*).

HURSLEY at Winchester (*Hants.*).

HURWORTH at Hutton Rudby (*Yorks.*).

ISLE OF WIGHT at Wareham (*I. of W.*).

EAST KENT at Aldington (*Kent*).

MID KENT STAGHOUNDS at Charing (*Kent*).

WEST KENT at Ightham (*Kent*).

LAMERTON at Kilworthy (*Devon*).

LANARKSHIRE AND RENFREWSHIRE at Houston (*Scotland*).

LAUDERDALE at Mosshouses (*Scotland*).

LEDBURY at Bushley Park (*Glos.*).

NORTH LEDBURY at Colwall Park (*Worcs.*).

LINLITHGOW AND STIRLINGSHIRE at Oatridge (*Scotland*).

LLANDILO FARMERS' at Cilmaenllwyd (*Carm.*).

LLANGEINOR at Penlynn (*Glam.*).

LLANGIBBY at Penhow (*Mon.*).

LUDLOW at Bromfield (*Salop*).

MELTON HUNT CLUB at Garthorpe (*Leics.*).

MENDIP FARMERS' at Nedge (*Som.*).

MEYNELL at Aston-on-Trent (*Derby*).

MIDDLETON AND MIDDLETON EAST at Whitwell on the Hill (*Yorks.*).

MINEHEAD HARRIERS AND WEST SOMERSET at Holmcote (*Devon*).

MODBURY HARRIERS at Wrangaton (*Devon*).

MONMOUTHSHIRE at Llanrapley (*Mon.*).

MORPETH at Pole Hill (*Northumberland*).

NEWMARKET AND THURLOW at Moulton (*Suffolk*).

NORTH NORFOLK HARRIERS at Bawdeswell (*Norfolk*).

WEST NORFOLK at Lexham (*Norfolk*).

NORWICH STAGHOUNDS at Hethersett (*Norfolk*).

SOUTH NOTTINGHAMSHIRE at Cropwell Bishop (*Notts.*).

OAKLEY at Newton Bromswold (*Beds.*).

SOUTH OXFORDSHIRE at Crowell (*Oxon.*).

OXFORD UNIVERSITY at Wroughton (*Wilts.*).

OXFORD UNIVERSITY BULLINGDON CLUB at Crowell (*Oxon.*).

PEGASUS CLUB (BAR) and KING'S TROOP R.H.A. at Kimble (*Bucks.*).

PEMBROKESHIRE at Scoveston Fort (*Pembs.*).

SOUTH PEMBROKESHIRE at Lydstep (*Pembs.*).

PENDLE FOREST AND CRAVEN HARRIERS at Sawley (*Lancs.*).

PENTYRCH at Pentyrch (*Glam.*).

PERCY, WEST PERCY AND MILVAIN at Ratcheugh (*Northumberland*).

PORTMAN at Badbury Rings (*Dorset*).

PUCKERIDGE at Bishops Stortford (*Herts.*).

PYTCHLEY at Guilsborough (*Northants.*).

WOODLAND PYTCHLEY at Dingley (*Northants.*).

QUORN at Cropwell Bishop (*Leics.*).

RADNOR AND WEST HEREFORDSHIRE at Bredwardine (*Radnor*).

ROCKWOOD HARRIERS at Bretton (*Yorks.*).

ROMNEY MARSH at East Guldeford (*Sussex*).

ROSS HARRIERS at Belmont (*Hereford*).

ROYAL ARTILLERY, Salisbury Plain at Larkhill (*Wilts.*).

ROYAL ENGINEERS DRAGHOUNDS at Bredhurst (*Kent*).

SANDHURST FOXHOUNDS AND STAFF COLLEGE DRAGHOUNDS at Tweseldown (*Hants.*).

NORTH SHROPSHIRE at Eyton-on-Severn (*Salop*).

SOUTH SHROPSHIRE at Eyton-on-Severn (*Salop*).

SILVERTON at Shobrooke (*Devon*).

SUMINGTON at Oswaldkirk (*Yorks.*).

WEST SOMERSET VALE at Nedge (*Som.*).

SOUTHDOWN at Ringmer (*Sussex*).

SOUTH POOL HARRIERS at Capton (*Devon*).

SOUTH WOLD at Revesby (*Lincs.*).

SPARKFORD VALE HARRIERS at King-weston (*Som.*).

SPOONER'S at Kilworthy (*Som.*).

NORTH STAFFORDSHIRE at Mucklestone (*Staffs.*).

SOUTH STAFFORDSHIRE at Fradley (*Staffs.*).

STAINTONDALE at Hawsker (*Yorks.*).

STEVENSTONE at Cranford (*Devon*).

SUFFOLK at Moulton (*Suffolk*).

OLD SURREY AND BURSTOW at Edenbridge (*Kent*).

SURREY UNION at Tisman's (*Surrey*).

EAST SUSSEX at Ringmer (*Sussex*).

TAUNTON VALE FOXHOUNDS at Jordans (*Som.*).

TEDWORTH at Larkhill (*Wilts.*).

TEME VALLEY at Brampton Bryan (*Radnor*).

TETCOTT at Bradworthy (*Cornwall*).

SOUTH TETCOTT at Wadlands (*Cornwall*).

TICKHAM at Lynsted (*Kent*).

TIVERTON FOXHOUNDS at Shobrooke (*Devon*).

TIVERTON STAGHOUNDS at Loosebeare (*Devon*).

TIVYSIDE at Lantyben (*Pembs.*).

TORRINGTON FARMERS' at Cranford (*Devon*).

TREDEGAR FARMERS' at Bassaleg (*Mon.*).

TYNEDALE at Corbridge (*Northumberland*).

UNITED at Brampton Bryan (*Salop*).

UNITED SERVICES at Larkhill (*Wilts.*).

VALE OF CLETTWR at Pencader (*Carms.*).

VALE OF LUNE HARRIERS at Whittington (*Lancs.*).

V.W.H. (CRICKLADE) at Wroughton (*Wilts.*).

V.W.H. (EARL BATHURST'S) at Siddington (*Glos.*).

VINE at Hackwood Park (*Hants.*).

WARWICKSHIRE at Wellesbourne (*Warwicks.*).

NORTH WARWICKSHIRE at Alcester (*Warwicks.*).

WEST WARWICKSHIRE FARMERS' at Alcester (*Warwicks.*).

WAVENEY VALLEY HARRIERS at Bawdeswell (*Norfolk*).

WESTERN at Porthleven (*Cornwall*).

WESTON HARRIERS at Wolvershill (*Som.*).

WEST STREET at Ramsgate Airport (*Kent*).

WHADDON CHASE at Great Horwood (*Bucks.*).

WHEATLAND at Wilbrighton (*Salop*).

WILTON at Badbury Rings (*Wilts.*).

The West Warwickshire Farmers' Hunt Point-to-Point.

SOUTH AND WEST WILTS. at Badbury Rings (*Wilts.*).

WORCESTERSHIRE at Upton-on-Severn (*Worcs.*).

WYLYE VALLEY at Larkhill (*Wilts.*).

SIR WILLIAM WATKIN-WYNN'S at Malpas (*Cheshire*).

YORK AND AINSTY (North and South) at Acomb (*Yorks.*).

ZETLAND at Marwood (*Durham*).

The British
Pony Society

British Show Jumping
Association

B.R.S.A.

B.F.S.S.

C.C.

ANIMAL HEALTH TRUST, 14 Ashley Place, S.W.1.

ARAB HORSE SOCIETY, Beechmead, Rowledge, Farnham, Surrey.

BRITISH DRIVING SOCIETY, 16 Bedford Square, London, W.C.1.

BRITISH FIELD SPORTS SOCIETY, 51 Victoria Street, London, S.W.1.

BRITISH HORSE SOCIETY, 16 Bedford Square, London, W.C.1.

BRITISH PERCHERON HORSE SOCIETY, Owen Webb House, Gresham Road, Cambridge.

BRITISH RIDING CLUBS, 16 Bedford Square, London, W.C.1.

BRITISH RIDING SCHOOLS ASSOCIATION, 33 Woodford Road, London, E.18.

BRITISH SHOW HACK AND COB ASSOCIATION, 16 Bedford Square, London, W.C.1.

BRITISH SHOW JUMPING ASSOCIATION, 16 Bedford Square, London, W.C.1.

BRITISH SHOW PONY SOCIETY, Church Cottage, Forest Row, Sussex.

CLEVELAND BAY HORSE SOCIETY, Midge Hall, Roxby, Staithes, Yorkshire.

CLYDESDALE HORSE SOCIETY, 19 Hillington Gardens, Glasgow, S.W.2.

COACHING CLUB, 16 Bedford Square, London, W.C.1.

DALES PONY IMPROVEMENT SOCIETY, Hollin Hill Farm, Hamsterley, Bishop Auckland, Co. Durham.

DARTMOOR PONY SOCIETY, Lower Hisley, Lustleigh, Newton Abbot, Devon.

ENGLISH CONNEMARA PONY SOCIETY,

H.I.S.

British Horse Society

N.P.S.

Animal Health Trust

B.P.H.S.

The Quinta, Bentley, Farnham, Surrey.

EXMOOR PONY SOCIETY, Gapland Orchard, Hatch Beauchamp, Taunton, Som.

FELL PONY SOCIETY, Packway, Windermere, Westmorland.

HACKNEY HORSE SOCIETY, 16 Bedford Square, London, W.C.1.

HIGHLAND PONY SOCIETY, 32 Rutland Square, Edinburgh.

HUNTERS IMPROVEMENT AND NATIONAL LIGHT HORSE BREEDING SOCIETY, 17 Devonshire Street, London, W.1.

JOINT MEASUREMENT SCHEME, 16 Bedford Square, London, W.C.1.

MASTERS OF FOXHOUND ASSOCIATION, 51 Victoria Street, London, S.W.1.

MASTERS OF HARRIERS AND BEAGLES ASSOCIATION, 51 Victoria Street, London, S.W.1.

NATIONAL PONY SOCIETY, 17 Devonshire Street, London, W.1.

NEW FOREST PONY BREEDING AND CATTLE SOCIETY, Deeracres, Lisle Court, Lymington, Hants.

PONY CLUB, 16 Bedford Square, London, W.C.1.

ROYAL AGRICULTURAL SOCIETY OF ENGLAND, 35 Belgrave Square, London, S.W.1.

ROYAL COLLEGE OF VETERINARY SURGEONS, 9 Red Lion Square, London, W.C.1.

SHETLAND PONY SOCIETY, 61 George Street, Perth.

SHIRE HORSE SOCIETY, 17 Devonshire Street, London, W.1.

SUFFOLK HORSE SOCIETY, 6 Church Street, Woodbridge, Suffolk.

WELSH PONY AND COB SOCIETY, Queen's Road, Aberystwyth, Wales.

YORKSHIRE COACH HORSE SOCIETY, amalgamated with the Cleveland Bay Horse Society.

IVEAGH
HARRIERS

MEYNELL
FOXHOUNDS

GLAMORGAN
FOXHOUNDS

WEST MEATH
FOXHOUNDS

ATHERSTONE
FOXHOUNDS

WELL-KNOW

PLAS MACHYNLLETH
FOXHOUNDS

DUKE OF BEAUFORT'S
FOXHOUNDS

BADSWORTH
FOXHOUNDS